Let's Not Lose Them

Suzanne Ferris

Let's Not Lose Them
Endangered Species in Australia

GP

Let's Not Lose Them: Endangered Species in Australia
ISBN 978 1 76109 477 4
Copyright © text Suzanne Ferris 2023
Cover image: Carole Helman

First published 2023 by
GINNINDERRA PRESS
PO Box 3461 Port Adelaide 5015
www.ginninderrapress.com.au

Contents

Dedication

This book seeks to reach out to more people, to increase our knowledge, love and respect for fellow creatures whose existence is now seriously at risk, largely through human activity, to raise awareness of how their survival and ours are interconnected. And, of course, to encourage more helpful engagement in our rescue work.

I am grateful to many people who have helped and encouraged me with the writing of *Let's Not Lose Them* – too many to list, so accept my thanks here. A few I must name: Felicity Jackson, Geraldine Garoni, Denise Konson, Marg Thomas, Vivienne Jones, Carole Helman, Phil Henley and, of course, my partner, Jeremy Barrett, for his tireless support, both practical and emotional.

I dedicate this book as a contribution to the wonderful work of our Australian environmental organisations whose dedicated staff work tirelessly to help save our threatened native animal species and the specific habitats they need in order to survive.

All proceeds received by the author from the sale this book will support the following:

Australian Conservation Foundation
Australian Wildlife Conservancy
Nature Conservancy NSW
Australian Marine Conservancy.

Introduction

Sometimes I wonder if echidnas ever suffer the same delusion humans have, that their species is the intelligent centre of the universe.

Sandtalk by Tyson Yunka Porta

When my partner and I moved up to the mid-north coast of NSW recently, I was keenly aware that climate change was no longer a mere threat but was already making its presence felt in alarming ways worldwide. How could I not be? Recent scientific studies have shown that, since the Agricultural Revolution roughly began roughly 11,000 years ago, the vegetation biomass has halved, human activity having altered almost two-thirds of the earth's land surface. Statistically, Australia leads the world in its biodiversity loss and consequent extinction of native species.

In Australia, a staggering 7.2 million hectares of threatened species habitat have disappeared, much of it to logging, but – surprisingly – even more to expanded European farming. Soon after moving to this enchanted place with its rich diversity of flora and fauna, I became concerned that so many of the creatures here, and their natural habitats, were seriously in trouble from the combined impact of logging, bushfires and development, as well as farming and all the other forms of human behaviour which are fuelling climate change.

I learned that many native species' numbers here are in decline; some already on the edge of extinction. I wanted to do something to help. But what? At eighty, the full-on activist role was not a realistic option. So I decided to write about the situation.

Given the numerous environmental scientists publishing works on every aspect of climate change, it felt audacious of me to think I might have anything to contribute. But I thought about all those people in cities and suburbs, leading busy lives which leave them little time to explore the natural world, and it came to me. I would write for them (and their children, too) as one layperson to another, in a series of essays which are easily accessible and each complete in itself. My hope is that this modest book might open new eyes to the beauty and uniqueness of some of the creatures whose very existence is increasingly tenuous, just as my eyes were opened as a result of moving here.

We happen to live in a special environment on the mid-north coast, but every location is enriched by something of the natural world if we tune in to it. Australia is one of twelve mega-diverse countries which together contain roughly 75% of earth's total biodiversity. But our politicians are failing shamefully to protect our natural world from the now increasingly drastic impacts of climate change. As recently as October 2021, Australian Conservation Foundation biodiversity adviser Brendan Sydes commented that Australians would be shocked to hear our federal government had opted to focus on a recovery plan for a mere 100 of our 1,900 or so species currently threatened, even as it throws huge sums of money at expanding exploitative and extractive industries.

Our dedicated environmental scientists are doing all they can. Whenever a species is found to be struggling to survive, scientists and generous volunteers rally to its aid, researching the causes and rescuing as many creatures as they can. Places such as Taronga Zoo, Melbourne Zoo, the Koala Rescue Hospital in Port Macquarie, the Solitary Islands Marine Park and adjoining Australian Marine Park Reserve in Coffs Harbour, and many others, are doing their best to protect our precious species into the future. But the situation is complex.

Whereas vulnerable and even endangered creatures can often be protected *in situ* or in simulated habitat, those which manage to survive unfortunately often become conservation-dependent because there is no healthy, appropriate habitat into which they can be released. The catch is – as these conservationists are well aware – that this can only be a temporary measure. At some point they need to be released back into the wild. But unless that wild habitat is maintained or restored, release will not offer them a future.

Scientists carrying out rescue work in the vast areas devastated during the wildfires of 2019–2020 are doing their utmost to improve the situation, but the task is obviously enormous. Nor is this event a one-off. Without large-scale, urgent action against climate change, these fires will be the new norm and possibly even worse! But we can't give in to this! Change *is* starting to happen, though noticeably *not* in the ranks of the two major political parties. Politicians are not providing the action we need; nor will they, as long as they receive huge donations from the very corporations and vested interests which are the main causes of the planetary crisis.

As a non-scientist, statistics are not my forte, but a few broad facts can help provide a big-picture context. For example, knowing that many of our species go back about fifty-five million years, to when Australia's separation from Antarctica was almost complete, and that by fifty-three million years ago, our continent had drifted towards the more tropical north, is important in explaining the uniqueness of much of our flora and fauna.

That descendants of creatures of such antiquity and uniqueness are alive today is awe-inspiring. I read recently that, in the mere 250 years since European invasion here, one in three of our unique mammals is now at risk of extinction, and of the mammals which existed at the time of this first European occupancy, 10% are already extinct. Given the interdependence of all creatures, a similar loss can be assumed across the whole web of biodiversity. This is horrifying. I don't have figures concerning other species like reptiles, marine life, amphibians and insects – and of course, plants – but we can assume they too would be pretty alarming. A loss of both water and land plant species will generally occur in parallel because they all exist in an intricate balance.

We need to act with urgency and conviction, and each do all we can to stem this tragic trend. We can, I'm sure, if we care. We can't sit back and wait for politicians. This is life-rescue work. My aim here is simply to share with you some of my personal experiences and learning about our fellow creatures, aware that you may not have such easy access, or time, to wade through all the wonderful, detailed, informed writings that are now in the public domain.

I'm hoping this might be a starting point – enough to encourage you to read further, and – even better – to find time to venture into the natural world in search of first-hand experience. Some of it will be closer to home than you may realise. And there are ways we can all help, wherever we live. At some level, I think even the few remaining climate change deniers are aware that we live under a looming shadow which threatens us all. It can be hard to hold onto hope in such a situation, when we are being governed by politicians who avoid the challenge this calls for, pandering to the big exploiters for purely self-seeking reasons.

Rather, in the face of more extreme and more frequent weather events, our taxpayers' money is being assigned to new gas and oil projects and defence expenditure to supposedly help protect us from our enemies, though the reality is, I suspect, that armaments building is more likely to simply up the ante. It's hard not to despair when you think of the positive uses we could put this enormous funding towards. Don't let me get started!

Although in such a world it's hard to hang onto hope, we must support each other to fight despair. As Michael Mann explains in *The New Climate War*, it's a sense of urgency that enables agency, which leads to action. It makes sense. What we've found, especially since moving up to the mid-north coast, is that volunteering to help in any way with this crisis we all face has connected us with some quietly inspiring people. Negative emotions about the future of this planet of ours still catch us all out at times, but we're learning from our friends up here, and the many informed, passionately motivated writers whose books we read, that being active and supportive of one another makes a huge difference.

There's a book I've recently had read to me by my patient partner (I am now sight-impaired). Written collaboratively by prominent environmental change spokespeople Christiana Figueres and Tom Rivett-Carnac, *The Future We Choose* outlines so positively the ways in which we as individuals can push back against the insatiable consumerist disease we have all to some extent been infected by:

> Psychological studies have shown that mass consumption creates a bigger and bigger hole in our lives that we keep trying to fill.

Small doses of political satire can help too: we've just finally discovered the Shaun Micallef programme, for example! But I digress...

We humans actually *depend* on nature for our own healthy survival (pollination is one obvious example). This means that when we cause damage to any part of the intricate, delicate fabric of nature's biodiversity, it is not only other living plants and creatures which suffer; we also damage ourselves and our future existence. For me, this reality has recently become patently clear as I observe and talk with the well-informed people we live among here.

By becoming the dominant species, we have unwittingly severed the vital thread which binds us into the natural world. As our species has become more sophisticated (not quite the word, but I can't think of a better one), our lives have become more and more distant from our natural one. As adults, most of us are unaware of our disconnection. Yet its absence seems to be a kind of grief for a deep-seated loss. I realised this for myself unexpectedly, for example, about a year ago.

Concrete-loving neighbours were preparing their building site with heavy machinery and much shouting. There was a small clump of mature eucalypts on their land which they set about felling. There was loud chainsawing then, all of a sudden, an ear-splitting crack and I found myself in unstoppable tears. I was aware of a piercing pain in my chest, as though my heart would burst. As though I *was* that tree! Maybe this sounds melodramatic, but it was real. And it's in all of us, that connection, whether we recognise it or not.

Getting older now, memories from early childhood are coming back more often. I remember lying on the grass watching ants tirelessly climbing up blades of grass and wondering why. I peered at cicadas I occasionally saw – usually dead, as they're well-concealed when alive – and was in awe of their beauty and puzzled by their loud-screeching chorus. And bird calls: what were they saying to one another? So many fellow creatures! Then life took over, and pretty much my only contact with living creatures was with horses, dogs and farm animals, apart from native creatures we saw on bushwalks in Victoria. It was the move up here which began the important reconnection. Because I've been luckier in this way than so many, I simply want to share something of the joy and wonder it has revitalised in me.

Claire Dunn (*Rewilding the Urban Soul)* puts this connectedness in a nutshell:

> Everything is what it is by virtue of its relationship with everything else.

Our loss of contact with our fellow creatures has been gradual, though there have been pivotal stages in human history during which we have increasingly distanced ourselves from the natural world we once shared with them. Put simply, the fundamental problem seems to have begun when humans first stopped seeing themselves as part of nature, and began to view nature as a vast resource there for their benefit, separate from themselves.

The Old Testament, for example, speaks from this assumption. For a long period of human history, this assumed dominance appeared sustainable, as our forebears began enclosing, cropping and grazing, clearing forested lands as they believed they needed to and raiding the seas for more than just survival needs (think whaling). But this approach has turned out to be finite. Today, it is obviously unsustainable.

The coming of the Industrial Revolution, barely two hundred years ago, coincided with rapid population growth. Convinced we were the clever species, we treated nature as existing purely for our use. With progress, our numbers grew – disproportionately to those of other living creatures, though our forebears were no doubt unaware of this trend at the time. In fairness, it *is* hard to see the big-picture scenario when we are immersed in it. And all this happened relatively gradually, unlike the rapid changes in our current world. We're all familiar with that saying: with the benefit of hindsight. And now the impact of climate change on the biodiversity of our planet is frighteningly apparent. We are *in* it.

My partner is reading to me in small bites from a book I encourage you to read for yourselves: *The Ascent of Humanity (Civilisation and the Human Sense of Self)* by Charles Eisenstein. I sigh with relief to hear such wisdom and big-picture awareness: at last, a voice that probes the deeper issues relating to how we humans behave and why, and how we have reached this critical point in evolutionary history.

The pivotal word in his thesis is separation, that it all began when our species became convinced we were superior to other creatures because we had the capacity to control and alter our world and, of course, that this gave us the unquestionable right. So ours has gradually become a world of clever technology and ego-driven exploitation. What I sense he will offer here is the insightful wisdom that is so desperately lacking right now. Reconnecting with our natural world is key to recovering what we have lost largely as a result of our own behaviour.

But don't get me wrong! I certainly don't want to be a messenger of doom, and it's clear that Eisenstein isn't arguing this. There is still so much we can do, both individually and collectively. Rediscovering that we are kin to all living creatures, including people whose cultures may seem alien to us, it is exciting to have our eyes opened to how much kinship we do all share.

Among researchers and writers exploring this is Professor Gisela Kaplan, a noted Australian animal scientist who has written extensively about primates and birds, and now focuses exclusively on Australian birds and their behaviour patterns. Again and again, she demonstrates observed behaviour patterns among various bird species which reveal some surprising – and mostly delightful! – skills and behaviours akin to ours: tool-making, food storage, empathy, pair-bonding and strategic planning, to mention just a few.

Let me share a recent, relevant personal experience. About five weeks ago, a pair of welcome swallows finally committed to their chosen nest-site in our courtyard, cleverly using a disused wasp nest as a solid foundation. We were not surprised: they'd been flying in and out for weeks as we sat there having breakfast. Every day for just over two weeks, the two of them put in long hours each day collecting building materials, weaving them skilfully into the mud they gathered to create something remarkably like a human mud-brick building. Their teamwork was something some of us could learn from!

The next phase involved one of them sitting on the eggs while the other fetched food for its partner. Finally, we knew they'd hatched because both parents were flat out keeping up the food supplies, and my partner caught a glimpse of a couple of tiny beaks. It was so exciting! Then today, returning home from our morning walk having finally spotted a pod of humpback whale cows and calves, we arrived to find two fragile little hatchlings lying on the stone floor, their tiny beaks opening and shutting feebly. My partner fetched the ladder, climbed up, and replaced the two helpless creatures into the nest, avoiding human touch. The parents actually returned and appeared to be feeding them again. We felt almost reassured. Almost.

There had been a couple of kookaburras hanging about, making me suspicious.

'Don't be silly,' said my partner. 'They'd have eaten the babies.'

But what if there had been more? When one bold kooka came in close, I waved my arms at him furiously, but I had to come right up to him before he deigned to move.

The two tiny fledglings we returned to the nest survived the night, but by about nine o'clock next morning we found three lying on the ground – this time, dead. It's a tough lesson in the way nature works. It occurs to me now that perhaps this is why many species give birth to more than they need to replace themselves. Think of turtles, which hatch in their hundreds, but are picked off as food by waiting predators as they make their desperate rush to the sea. How few survive! As a child, I wondered at such wastefulness; now I understand that the balance is all worked out in the complex biodiversity web, so that a species will reproduce enough for its own species' survival, plus excess numbers to supply food for creatures for whom it is appropriate diet.

I researched welcome swallows to learn that they will have two, and often three, attempts at replace themselves each year if earlier offspring have fallen prey to the food chain. And already our pair is swooping in and out of the courtyard, hopefully planning another attempt. It's a pity our species hasn't stuck to replacement only as our breeding principle now that medical knowledge and higher living standards have vastly improved survival rate in many countries. And that we consume more than we need and are only now broadly beginning to appreciate how much we actually depend on other species, both flora and fauna.

We need to rediscover the truth that we are part of nature, as First Peoples here and elsewhere have traditionally known. We descendants of the early invaders are increasingly learning about and from our own Indigenous peoples about caring for Country sustainably. I have found, both at a personal level and more generally, that our First Peoples are not only deeply knowledgeable about this ancient and complex environment, but show remarkable forgiveness and generosity of spirit in sharing it. Their practices in land management and the way they used fire as a strategy are cases in point. Dr Wayne Webb, a Pibulmun Wadandi Yungunjarli elder, explained to *The Saturday Paper* (October 2021),

> In my culture, everything has a voice, a right to exist, and it's time we really stood and listened because without water nothing survives, without oxygen nothing survives, and without our biodiversity working together our planet, our Earth, our culture and our people cannot live.

It's encouraging that environmentalists, both white and Indigenous, now increasingly work together.

That our precious biodiversity is now under severe threat is indisputable. To illustrate the point, here are a few recent statistics concerning native species in Australia and the percentage currently listed as at risk: mammals 21%; birds 17%; reptiles 21%; amphibians 22%. Similar statistics apply to marine creatures, while the percentage of insects at risk in Australia is an alarming 40% – many of them being species we haven't even identified.

Perhaps you've noticed that driving on country roads doesn't collect the carnage of grasshoppers and other insects on your windscreen and front grille that it used to? Perhaps you don't see as many bees and butterflies in your garden as you used to? And you can be sure there will be a corresponding decline in the numbers of the creatures who depend on them for food, and on those they themselves need as food. The message is unmistakable: nature is in trouble, and mainly from human behaviour.

My current research project began with the Bellinger River snapping turtle. Before we arrived in Bellingen, these small amphibians had been discovered to be in grave trouble. Roughly ninety of their dead bodies had been found floating on the surface of the river on 1 February 2015. Reading about these turtles, I learned the species is millions of years old. It's a shock to discover that now these small creatures are threatened with possible extinction and in desperate need of our help. As I read, I became increasingly aware of the extraordinary interconnectedness of all living things.

I read some up-to-date statistics that might surprise you, supplied by the Clean Air and Urban Development Landscapes Hub – an organisation you might consider joining if you want to play a voluntary conservation role. Of the roughly 30% of environmentally protected flora and fauna species in Australia, more of them are actually concentrated in our cities and suburbs than in rural areas. In fact, 39% of the at-risk species occur only in urban areas. So you can see how important and rewarding it can be to become involved in saving our native species right where you live! They are an essential part of your community. Sadly, 56% of our species are already absent from some urban locations: for instance, the growling grass frog (ACT, NSW and Victoria) has declined sharply in numbers over the past ten years, and is now found only in small, isolated pockets.

On the other hand, living in cities, suburbs or semi-rural villages can give us an inflated impression of the survival rate of our native animal and insect species. Living as my partner and I do in a small coastal, subtropical settlement situated in a forested region, we see plenty of birdlife in particular – indeed, if anything, the numbers appear to have increased since the wild-fire devastation of 2019–2020.

Commenting about this to long-time locals, we learned the reason: many birds whose habitats were destroyed by the fire have flocked to similar habitats not affected – that is, to more built-up areas closer in. You may also have noticed this and assumed, as we initially did, that their numbers were healthy. Sadly, this is not usually the case. And the huge fire event of 2019–20 isn't the only reason – merely an exacerbating one – though it may be the biggest wake-up call, since it cost the lives of an estimated three billion creatures.

According to Sir David Attenborough, tropical rainforests are the most terrestrially diverse land environments in the world, though the marine ecology is even more diverse because it not only covers more of the planet's surface, but has depth as well. Here in the temperate subtropical mid-north coast, we experience high rainfall, and are blessed with vast coastal and river waterways, but also a mix of wet and dry sclerophyll forest and heath country in the adjacent hinterland and mountain regions.

Given this range of habitats, it is hardly surprising that we enjoy such rich wildlife diversity. Located between the temperate and the tropical zones, seasons here are typically less distinctly marked than, say, where we formerly lived in central Victoria, so plant growth doesn't suffer much seasonal setback. Like everywhere on the planet, though, seasonal patterns are becoming less predictable. Many changes are taking place in our natural habitats everywhere, causing some of our flora and fauna to travel further afield in search of their specific environmental needs.

The Black Summer fire event has had a devastating effect on all the regions it savaged. And it's hardly surprising that species which were already vulnerable or endangered fared worst during these terrifying months. In this region, two examples will illustrate the point. The powerful owl losses were increased by 54% in the burnt areas, and the little rufus scrub bird – classified as 'vulnerable' before these fires – lost a further 75% in burnt areas and 47% in areas not actually destroyed by fire. It may well now be extinct. The swift parrot is another – and the list could go on.

The tragic plight of so many of our koalas has, of course, been widely covered in the media. Also not surprising is the fact that the smaller animal and bird species are usually those most affected by severe bushfire, not only because they can't travel as fast or far, but because they tend to inhabit lower-vegetated environments. After the fires, too, the exposed ground makes them easy prey for equally -hungry predators to pick off.

Why do we need to save our threatened flora and fauna worldwide, some might still ask? Extinction, after all, is a natural process. This is true, of course, but without the massive human intervention in nature's cycle, studies show that the pace of evolutionary change was so gradual it was barely perceptible.

According to David Attenborough, extinction is now happening a hundred times faster than it did just a hundred years ago, and we seem to be the cause. That's an alarming statistic! It's not hard to detect the tone of deep concern in his voice, even from the printed page. Another reason for action to save our native species: we care. There's something uniquely precious about looking into the eyes of another creature in its natural habitat. A kind of kinship recognition takes place, I think.

Watch Attenborough meeting and engaging with gorillas (his DVDs and YouTubes are easy to track down) and the connection, the mutual recognition, is unmistakable. With smaller creatures, the connection can be less obvious, but it's always there. We are part of nature, not owners of it; these are our kin.

As Attenborough points out, if we don't dramatically change our exploitative ways now as a real priority, we as a species could well be facing the end of life as we know it in the foreseeable future. The planet itself would survive, he points out, and other species of flora and fauna would recover in one form or another, once our heavy hand is removed. But he ends on a positive note, highlighting the many ways in which, both individually and collectively, we can make meaningful changes in the way we choose to live and engage with our natural world. This is not the place to launch into detail: read *A Life on Our Planet*.

It seems more appropriate here to mention some of the many projects under way globally, aimed at preserving species biodiversity. For instance, there is a national goal in Australia of rescuing ten of our threatened marsupial species.

In far south-western NSW, the tiny numbat, thought for the past hundred years to be extinct here, has been bred in captivity. Four females and one male have already been released into a predator-free habitat and, once their numbers are greater, will be released back into the wild, provided there is suitable, healthy habitat – a huge change in itself.

In Tasmania, Bob Brown has been fighting a determined legal battle to preserve important habitat for the critically endangered swift parrot; a similar battle is occurring in Victoria on behalf of the beautiful leadbeater possum. It needs to be said, though, that all the wonderful conservation efforts of individual and official conservation organisations (think of Taronga Zoo in Sydney, for one) to prevent extinction can only be effective where there is appropriate habitat for them to be released into.

A life in permanent captivity is not really a solution. With climate change-driven events growing in frequency and severity, this can be problematic. Hence the urgent need for effective climate action by us, the people. We can't wait any longer for recalcitrant governments.

Exciting new environmental science research is emerging. Examples include: drone-fertilising and pesticide spreading – automatic, and considerably cheaper than traditional practices; low interest-rate loans from banks for farmers transitioning to sustainable farming; the production of plant-based macronutrients to reduce the energy-guzzling effects of extensive meat production; and the invention of mechanical bee pollinators, which will be discussed in the bee chapter. And these trends will increase as more and more people get it.

Climate change and the increasing damage it is causing to all life on this planet is without doubt the hot issue (pun intended). No wonder so many scientists and high-profile writers and activists worldwide are turning their attention to this central topic. Names like Tim Flannery, Jared Diamond, Bruce Pascoe, Ian Lowe, Michael Mann, along with others such as Naomi Klein, Al Gore, Bill McKibben, David Suzuki, Greta Thunberg and earlier writers with foresight like Rachel Carson. Even as I write these names, more concerned, informed writers and environmentalists are publishing their pleas to add to the mounting sense of urgency.

Just recently, I watched a thirty-eight-minute joint interview between David Attenborough and Greta Thunberg (the young Swedish activist). It brought tears to my eyes listening to the deep passion and wisdom from these two – the voices of youth and age connecting like bookends in their combined plea for this planet and its embattled natural world.

David Attenborough, for me, combines the knowledge, humility, sanity, deep conviction, wisdom and passion we need right now to embrace the challenges of this critical point in human history.

Greta, a small, gifted teenager with an Asperger's condition which – far from being an impediment – gives inspired 'fire' and focus to the fearless voice with which she challenges us all. Look up her address to the 2020 Summit Conference which begins: 'Our house is on fire!' if you haven't already. Listening to this teenager boldly confronting the power-brokers of the world who are effectively blocking a sane, ethical response to what we all now face, made me thrill with pride that our species *can* produce such amazing people.

If you live in an urban environment, as we both did for many years, the issue of climate change may feel a little remote, experienced mainly through a summer of more uncomfortably hot days, though news coverage about more frequent and extreme flooding is making it apparent that climate events are no longer mainly a problem for farmers.

We all followed the news coverage of extreme weather of the 2019–2020 wildfires and flash flooding as almost surreal spectacles, but they're looming closer and closer to us all. It takes on a whole new dimension when we experience these horrors in our immediate environments, and witness the effects of climate change (wildfire, floods, cyclones, extreme-heat days) on our fellow creatures and their natural environments, some of which can never fully recover.

We are lucky to have people who care and act, like the volunteers and experts working to save burnt, scorched or orphaned koalas at the sanctuary-hospital in Port Macquarie. There are wonderful projects being carried out here and elsewhere to switch to regenerative farming and, as farmers let go of large-scale grazing, setting aside more land for re-wilding. As Attenborough demonstrates, if we stop extractive farming, nature will do its own regenerating – and surprisingly quickly.

Most of us are instinctively drawn more towards living creatures than to their habitats. I've included native bees in this selection: where would we be without our precious pollinators? And I hope to show that it's a similar story with spiders. But the symbiotic relationship that exists between each living creature (whether herbivore or carnivore) and its essential habitat is vital.

Something I've observed in human behaviour – which may well have occurred to you too – is that we *are* drawn to other creatures and even thrill to a sense of connection with creatures with whom we can make eye contact. Yet when it comes to our own species, we tend to do the opposite: to latch onto the petty difference (race, religion, political and gender preferences and so on), ignoring the huge common ground we share. Over time, this has led us to the point where, unless we can face this reality and learn to pull together, our future as a species on this wonderful planet is seriously under threat. We need to be aware of this overhanging cloud, but to focus on what we *can* do to avert this course. There is still hope – but there is a time pressure.

As we're aware now, our long-inherited assumption that humans are the superior species, the lords of creation, has led us over many hundreds of years to gradually disrupt the balance of nature to the point where, quite suddenly it seems, nature is rebelling in an alarming way with extreme events like cyclones, savage and increasingly frequent wildfires and massive flooding, and now a pandemic as well. In this context of human dominance, it's curious that there is a tendency to sentimentalise, to anthropomorphise some of our cute fellow creatures (koalas are a classic Australian example).

The healthier and more rewarding approach is surely to learn about the complexities of individual species and the many ways in which they resemble us. They are, after all, our kin. Those special occasions when we are lucky enough to eyeball one of our fellow beings seems to me like proof. (Maybe looking a fish in the eye is a slight stretch, though not a refutation, I suggest.)

There are so many ways we can all become nature-supporters. For instance, if you have any garden space, you can create an indigenous garden (and don't forget the roof garden option if you live in high-density inner city: this is proving exciting and productive for increasing numbers of people) to attract native bees, lizards and birds as well as the tiny creatures which will also be tempted to make their homes with you. We collected some small logs cut from a fallen branch and stood them upright in a secluded spot with holes drilled in the sides for solitary (native) bees to occupy. Six months later, we now have bees in quite a few of them.

Having a water source is good, too – especially as the summer heat gets harder and harder for small creatures to survive. Butterflies and bees – even flies – need water, just as we do. Now that logging and burnt-out forest habitats are being destroyed at alarming rates, our fellow creatures are becoming more dependent on those of us who live in built-up areas. And don't forget that *we* need *them* too – as I hope to show in these essays.

We also chose to omit the old-fashioned lawn – a tradition brought here by early colonists, inappropriate for this country, especially now. Using mulch and gravel and rocks not only uses less water and labour, but also provides a more inviting place to share with our fellow creatures. I love that Indigenous term for lawns: white-man desert.

Moving up here has been a huge wake-up call for us. Among other things, it has prompted me to write this volume of essays in the hope that it might whet your appetite too, so that you might read more widely and deeply into this critical situation we all face. And better still, it might tempt you to venture into the natural world yourself to experience how awe-inspiring it is. To sense how connected we all are with the amazing ecosystem of which we are a part.

A Delicate Balance

Imagine: 1840 in the Bellingen Valley – mid-north coast, NSW, as we call it today. Summer, warm and humid. There's been a storm…lush vegetation gleams in the sunlight. Shrieks of laughter rise from the river as the children splash happily in its pristine waters. A couple of lean, supple young men stand quietly further up the river with spears poised ready to catch passing fish. Birds join in – plaintive yellow-tailed black cockatoos, lyrical butcherbirds, the reverberating crack of darting whip birds, a noisy flock of gaudy rainbow lorikeets…so much vibrant activity, coming alive in the glistening foliage after the storm. The whole valley teems with life.

The children are Gumbaynggirr. For thousands of years, their people have dwelt in semi-permanent shelters near the Bellinger River, thriving in harmony with the healthy climate. The region's waters and forests provide rich, varied food supplies: a well-balanced mix of fruits, nuts, vegetables, meat and fish. The women gather nuts, fruits, seeds, roots and berries, as well as snakes, lizards, yabbies and other small water creatures. They also do some of the fishing, though it is the men who hunt bigger animals and catch the abundant marine life, the larger fish, eels and turtles, using canoes made from the curved bark of stringybark trees. The women make baskets and other utensils. They cook and mind the younger children communally. Around the campfire at night, the stories are told.

For so long, they have been living this way, never disturbing the delicate balance of nature. For Indigenous people, the land is their mother, with whom they have a deep, spiritual bond. Of course, they are few in number – there were only about three hundred Gumbaynggirr occupying the Bellingen Valley when settlers first arrived. No doubt their

Fishing in the Bellinger River (etching, early 1840s).

varied diet included the unique Bellinger River snapping turtle (BRST),
but in such small numbers that the species continued to flourish
throughout this vast period.

The variety of tree and plant species then was boundless. Forest trees
included the white booyong, ficus, *Cryptocaria* (*oblata*, for example),
grey myrtle, laurina, waterhousia, red cedar, and numerous varieties of
melaleuca and eucalypt – the latter including blackbutts, grey gums and
tallowwoods. Among the smaller, shrubby plants were the blade-leaved
cordylines, and what are commonly called walking stick palms with
their dramatic hanging displays of red berries.

I first saw the latter in nearby Dorrigo National Park and was not
surprised to find them appearing in some of my rainforest paintings. It
must have been almost impossible to walk through these dense forests
in their original state. The scrambling vines that remain today twist and
writhe around other plants, somehow leaping from one tree trunk to
another, monkey-wise, often several metres apart, and can be challenging to the walker. Giant pepper vines, water vines, lawyer vines – a long
list – even today can be seen hanging loosely in the upper levels. Add
to this the forbs: the multitude of forest-floor species like rat's tail orchid

Bellingen rainforest.

(*Dendrobium gracilicaule*). Specimens of this can mostly be found today in the Bellingen Valley, though in depleted numbers.

We rely on visual representations such as the one at the start of this chapter, and descriptions in diary and documentary records made by the earliest white people to arrive here, along with a dash of imagination, inspired by what still remains of this idyllic valley, to visualise it in its pristine form. When the first white settlers set foot in this valley, we know that the river was deep and wide, bordered on either side by lush, subtropical forest and greenery coming right to the water's edge. As a backdrop, we still see the densely treed hills of the Great Escarpment, despite the forest logging which continues unabated.

This is the section of the Bellinger River which has been the marine and terrestrial habitat of the BRST as their unique natural environment. Their digestive systems responded favourably to its highly oxygenated water and low particulate load. The dietary requirements here were also ideally met. These turtles are omnivorous, with a slight preference for a carnivorous diet, so macro-invertebrates such as water beetles and dragonflies, along with frogs, supplied their base diet, supplemented by terrestrial fruit and aquatic vegetation. Eating both macro-invertebrates and rotting plant matter in the water, together with what was available on the banks and in the riparian zone, they have played an important cleansing role for the river. Correspondingly, the deep pools of clear water and continuous flow over a bedrock of boulders, pebbles and gravel for most of the year were perfect for their needs, as were the hidden rock ledges they needed for breeding purposes.

The arrival of the first white settlers (1841) into this idyllic place marks the point from which it all began to unravel – slowly and imperceptibly at first, no doubt. The key difference between Indigenous peoples and white settlers is that whereas our First Peoples lived interactively and respectfully with the rest of nature, the Europeans tended to regard nature as a resource to be exploited for their own use.

A case can be argued that the European assumption that the Earth existed for our species alone dates back to the Old Testament, where God exhorts Man to go forth and multiply, to fill the Earth and 'have dominion over it'. We seem to have done that!

But more accurately, it started with the Agrarian Revolution, which began roughly ten thousand years ago, when nature first began to be regarded as a resource for the human species as somehow above and supe-

Logging began once Hodgkinson discovered the cedar trees.

rior. This was mentioned in the introduction, and of course Christianity is only one of the belief systems to have had a shaping influence on human behaviour. But it was the dominant one among the first invaders into Australia. Today, the plight of the BRST can be seen as a definite casualty. Impact on this natural environment began in 1841: William Miles, a stockman from Kempsey, discovered this lush haven, then the same year government surveyor Clement Hodgkinson arrived here and soon recognised its red cedar-logging potential.

Logging of the magnificent red cedars started even before Bellingen began to be settled as a town. The absence of proper roads meant that logs had to float downstream about six kilometres to Fernmount. There they were loaded onto long rafts and shunted to Urunga, where the broad Bellinger and Kalang Rivers form a confluence to the Pacific Ocean. The entry point here was dredged, with large rock walls on either side to allow ocean-going ships to load the timber for export. During our house search in and around Bellingen, we inspected a house in Fernmount which had been built as a logging depot. Despite its magnificent tallowwood floorboards, we would have felt uncomfortable buying into such a sorry history.

This valley is still very beautiful, even in its altered form. Bellingen Shire, with its surrounding countryside and waterways, is considered one of Australia's richest natural environments, blessed with high rainfall, fertile soils, its rivers fed by tributary creeks which themselves rival our familiar, muddy Yarra in Melbourne, city of our birth. We moved to this paradise early in 2017.

Not long after we arrived, we noticed some faded posters around town advertising a Bellinger River Snapping Turtle Festival. The reason came as a shock: on 1 February 2015, at least ninety BRSTs had been found floating on the river, dead, close to the Never Never Creek catchment area. Curiosity prompted me to talk with environmentally switched-on locals. The more I heard, the more significant and tragic the story that emerged. The catalyst was a virus, but the backstory is more complex.

An article in the *Bellingen Courier Sun* (30 September 2015) stated,

The Bellingen River Snapping Turtle is now functionally extinct and can only be kept alive by human intervention.

A day later, it had been officially listed as critically endangered under the *Threatened Species Conservation Act, 1995* and the *Biodiversity Act, 1999*. The final tally totalled roughly four hundred and twenty known deaths. Before this, species numbers had apparently been abundant. Of the two three hundred left at that time, most were young, so it will be

Captive-bred Bellinger snapping turtles, Taronga Zoo.

years before they reach breeding age – that is, if they survive in the currently degraded habitat. This tragic loss is a significant indicator of adverse conditions in the riverine ecosystem. There seems to be a sad parallel between the fate of the BRSTs and that of the original human inhabitants here, the Gumbaynggir: both have had their ancient natural habitats seriously disrupted during the brief period since white settlement began.

The Bellinger River snapping turtle (*Myuchelis georgesi*) is unique to this specific stretch of our river, running from Ebor on the New England Tablelands through Dorrigo and Bellingen to Urunga where, together with the Kalang River, it enters the Pacific Ocean. The stretch of the Bellinger inhabited by the turtle has provided the perfect ecological environment for their needs for millions of years, existing in symbiotic harmony with its riverine habitat.

The name Bellingen itself is an anglicisation of the Gumbaynggirr *baligin* or *baalijin*, having various meanings and associations such as clear water winding river, quoll, or cheeky fellow. The general assumption is that the cheeky fellow actually refers to the quoll. A friend of mine camping at the Tarkine in Tasmania had her new, expensive sleeping bag chewed into by a quoll, so this seems to support that cheeky assumption!

Snapping turtles as a genus are certainly not unique to Bellingen or

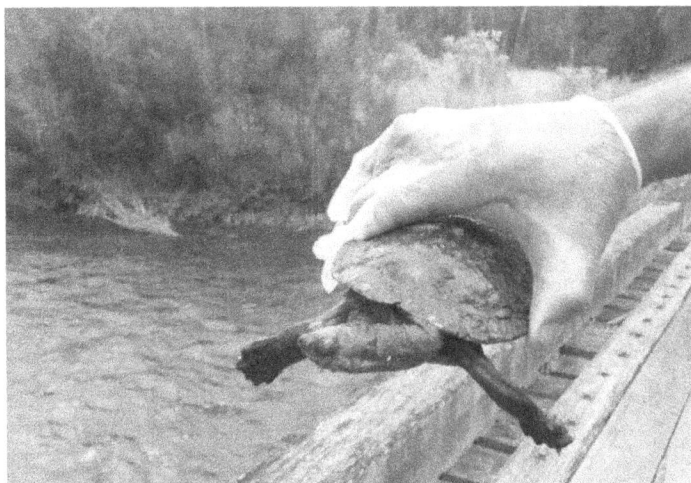

One of the many turtles found dead on the river, 1 February 2015.

even Australia. There are snapping turtles in other parts of the world too. A friend of mine who grew up in Maryland, USA, recalls being afraid to swim in the river on their farm because of the prevalence of snapping turtles there. But the Bellingen version is unique to this river.

They are small creatures: the shell of an adult fits into the palm of a fully opened hand. It must feel awe-inspiring to hold one of these strange creatures, knowing the ancient history of its gene pool.

Snapping turtles as a genus have a jagged shell edge; in the BRST this is confined to its serrated hind edge, whereas the later-introduced *Emydura macquarii* from Port Macquarie has a fully serrated shell. The latter, being hardier, appears not to have been afflicted by the virus. Apart from the serrated hind edge of the shell, our turtle has a beak-like mouth with two curious-looking barbels protruding from its chin. The legs are quite long in proportion to the shell size, with large webbed and clawed feet. Its neck, when extended, is long and almost snake-like.

The bulbous head features large, round, staring eyes framed by wrinkled circles. The snout is blue-tinged with a large pair of nostrils, the underside distinguished by clear, linear markings. The outer shell is also attractively patterned. Everything about it suggests antiquity: its wrinkled reptilian skin, its blunt features and round eyes with their hooded lids, its slow movements, all convey such a sense of ancient dignity. And of vulnerability.

Like the crocodile, the turtle dates back to prehistoric times. Recent palaeontological and morphological studies support the theory that it evolved, surprisingly, from crocodiles and birds, seemingly during the Permian Era aeons ago. Compared to them, we are newcomers who, judging by present indications, seem highly unlikely to endure as they have. The fact that we should be the major cause of this tragic mortality event is sadly ironic.

At the time of the 2015 mortality event, extensive testing was done to determine details of the viral attack. Dr Kirkland, a virologist with the NSW DPI, found that it was the same nidovirus which had attacked lizards and pythons, but in the case of the turtles, had caused kidney damage and total blindness. Genomic testing attributed this to their much higher concentrations of nucleotide.

Captive breeding programmes started almost immediately after the mortality event. Locally, a concerned group formed the Bellingen River-watch in February 2015. A very positive project soon started at Sydney's Taronga Zoo and has achieved promising breeding results: twenty-two hatchlings survived in 2017 and a further thirty-one the following year, making a total of fifty-three tiny BRSTs. The work continues, with some turtles having been released back into a section of the river in 2021. The survivors in the river, which are mainly young, are also being carefully tested and monitored.

But here is the other challenge of the project: healthy young turtles can't simply be released back into the degraded habitat where so many had died. Major work was carried out by a collaborative team of the Bellingen Shire Council, the Office of Environment and Heritage and Bellingen Landcare to have river and riparian zones ready for release of some of the captive-bred turtles by 2021.

The NSW Office of the Environment also set clear protocols regarding human care and respect for the health of the river. For example, the so-called secret of the Never-Never swimming holes has become widely known to tourists. A toilet block is desperately needed but for legal reasons relating to ownership of the land there, this can't happen. Human effluent has caused an alarmingly high E-coli count – good for neither humans nor turtles.

Many factors have contributed to the degradation of this Bellingen valley habitat, affecting both land and water. But clearly, climate change and related human activity are the main causes of deterioration to the river and its banks, to the point now of virtual extinction of the BRST – that is, requiring captive breeding to survive. It remains to be seen whether sustained life in the wild habitat can really be achieved, but it is vital that we try to achieve this.

Bellingen has traditionally had a high rainfall throughout most of the year, apart from its dry winters. This pattern is changing: lately, not only is the annual average decreasing, but it tends to fall more irregularly, with occasional large floods. The torrents of water during these floods tend to erode the banks, causing sedimentation and turbidity, a problem compounded by cattle going down to drink. Higher summer temperatures and an growing number of very hot days have also raised the water temperature during ur increasingly long summers.

Farming and grazing have contributed in other ways, too. Deforestation and clearing of riparian vegetation along the river flats to increase available grazing land for dairy cows has probably been counterproductive, even for the dairy farmers, from loss of weather protection for stock. Not only has this not improved stocking rates; it has been detrimental to the BRSTs' riparian environment. The increased water temperatures resulting from hotter summers have also caused evaporation of the deep, clear pools necessary for the turtles' health and breeding grounds.

Predation by other animals is another undermining factor: goannas and foxes, as well as feral dogs and cats, account for many deaths, especially of young turtles and nests, which are easy prey. This is compounded by the fact that most of the victims of the major virus attack were mature, breeding-age turtles.

Another compounding factor relates to the introduction into these waters of the hardier *Emydura macquarii*. Shortage of suitable food supplies is now favouring their survival over that of the more delicate indigenous turtles into whose habitat they have been introduced. Interbreeding between BRSTs and the hardy Macquarie River species hasn't helped either. Biodiversity conservation is about preserving unique creatures in their naturally evolved habitats. The tougher Macquarie River turtle will possibly dominate and threaten the survival of the unique BRST.

So this ancient species, only found in a particular section of the Bellinger River, has come close to being wiped out forever because both its environment and dietary requirements have been seriously compromised. And, as I hope I've already indicated, biodiversity and climate change are complex and interconnected; every living organism has a precise, reciprocal role in the whole scheme.

Human activities such as dairy farming and logging have damaged the health of the river water and riparian zones, making it therefore harder for the turtles to fulfil their purifying role. Therefore, the river system also suffers from the absence of their vital role as cleansing agents.

The importance of this creature to the ecosystem of the river is evidenced in the high E-coli count measures of the river water which followed after the sudden mortality event. These formerly pristine waters are now more sludgy and turbid, especially after heavy rain events. This obviously affects all living creatures and plant life there. The fact that the *Emydura maquarii* species appears to cope better with the situation further upsets this natural balance as an introduced species.

If this prehistoric little creature is to be saved, two main things need to happen. Though the captive breeding programme at Taronga Zoo is proving successful, with each year's hatchlings and the eggs from which they hatched are becoming more viable, the numbers are still very small. Being so young, too, it will be years before they themselves reach breeding age. But apart from this, breeding in captivity is only ever a salvaging strategy.

The other major project is to recreate the healthy, appropriate eco-environment in which to release them. The collaborative efforts of state and local bodies referred to earlier are endeavouring to achieve this for at least the upper reaches of the turtles' river habitat. If they succeed, this will be a promising start, but the project is huge: not only the river water but the riparian zone also needs to be cleared of weed and non-indigenous vegetation, then appropriately replanted and established.

Full restoration of the ecological balance, here as elsewhere, is no longer possible, but we urgently need to protect our precious environment from further degradation. The damage to this beautiful, richly endowed piece of Australia has crept up on us to a near-critical point. It evidently takes a catastrophic event like waking up one morning to find masses of dead turtles floating on the river, bloated, their blind eyes a pink haze, to shock us out of our complacency.

Change is an inevitable part of life. But human activity in Australia since colonisation has overwhelmed this natural cycle of adaptation to the extent that the countless other living things cannot keep up. More and more living plants and animals are facing possible extinction. The BRST is one example.

The fundamental reason this explosive ecological change coincided with the occupation by white settlers a mere two hundred and -fifty years ago can be attributed simply to a totally different understanding of what is meant by land. The ramifications are huge and complex.

The concept of land to the first peoples is deeply holistic and grounded in a culture we are now discovering is probably over sixty-five thousand years old. Country, as they call it, embodies spirit, culture, community and stories in a way that is inseparable from the earth, the sea and the sky.

Coming from a concept of land as property and a resource for human profit (think mining and agribusiness farming, for a start), it's a hard concept for non-Indigenous people like us to grasp.

I've just finished reading *First Knowledges* by Page and Memmott and it's given me at least some appreciation of how meaningful and relevant their relationship with Country must become for us to learn from today. As Lucy Turnbull says on the cover of the book,

> the need to tread lightly – to understand Country and its knowledge, has never been greater.

For thousands of years, the BRST existed in a symbiotic relationship that started to unravel from the 1840s, when Europeans began to alter the land. The exploitation of this precious habitat continued to the stage that we are now in urgent rescue mode. The first white settlers at this time were obviously unaware of the impact of their practices on this new, delicate environment (they tended, actually, to see it as harsh); they simply brought with them their familiar strategies. Today, we're becoming more acutely aware. More and more people are taking responsibility, actively attempting to avert what could be the extinction of unique species such as this tiny, ancient turtle. The BRST is one of a rapidly growing number of plant and animal species under threat. Our rich biodiversity is shrinking at an alarming rate.

We can't hope to bring back the past. But we can still slow the destructive process. We can fight for more sustainable logging practices, for a start.

Still a regular sight!

It may still be possible to rescue this precious turtle and recreate its healthy environment. This chapter, written by a non-scientist, is an attempt to raise awareness of the imminent crisis – one voice among many, though not enough. It's a plea for the rapidly growing numbers of plant and animal species now threatened by extinction.

Biodiversity loss is more subtle, less apparent, than climate change. All life is precious, and unless we come together to repair the damage our behaviour has caused, embracing the connectedness of the whole, with ourselves as part of it rather than continuing to control and exploit, life as we know it on our planet may become unsustainable.

Part of the problem is that too few people are lucky enough to be in regular contact with the natural world; living in cities and suburbs, nature barely impinges on their busy lives.

I recall a group of senior secondary students I worked with in Victoria planting native trees in the barren school grounds of the western suburbs on Friday afternoons.

'Yuk, Miss, how can you bear to touch that dirt?'

Beautiful kids! Just no contact with the natural world. We all need this and the sense of wonder it evokes. Now more than ever. What you've never known, you're unlikely to miss consciously, but you are, all the same, somehow spiritually impoverished. School students need to experience their natural world as young and as often as possible, through frequent camps, excursions, visual media and every means possible to encourage connectedness. They need to discover that soil is not dirt, to experience the awe that comes from looking into the eyes of other strange and beautiful fellow creatures, to see, touch and smell trees and plants, to hear the amazing range and complexity of bird calls and how they communicate. Climate, biodiversity and our role in it need to form a central part in the curriculum.

It's exciting to see students beginning to take the initiative themselves, perhaps initially inspired by Greta Thunberg, who wagged school in Sweden to shock people into awareness of the gravity of climate change. Her impact is now global and not only among students.

*Source of the Bellinger River: the falls at Piont Lookout,
south-west of Ebor.*

These students are not, as a certain forgettable politician described them, our future dole bludgers. They are future voters who are aware that our so-called leaders, driven by vested interests, are lying to us and failing our planet. Even in suburbs, changes such as rising temperatures and severe water restrictions are becoming increasingly hard to ignore.

Here, the BRST is an important wake-up call. Reflect that a small creature such as this, which we now know existed in the Triassic period of the Mesozoic era, should suddenly be facing likely extinction as a result of our activities in the short span of years settlers have occupied this place is surely shocking. We must take responsibility, get on board in whatever ways we can to rescue our unique and important fellow creatures.

Postscript

On 3 March 2021, seventeen of the captive-bred Bellinger River snapping turtles were released back into the Bellinger River where substantial riparian and water quality restoration work has been carried out. There have been two more releases since then, making a total of fifty-two.

They are being carefully monitored, and their carers will not release others until confident these turtles are thriving. Indications so far are positive.

Bats or Koalas?

If you were to ask most people, even today, which is the best known of Australia's native species, they would very likely say automatically either the kangaroo or the koala. If you asked for their spontaneous reaction at the mention of the flying fox, the reply might include words like dirty, smelly and disease-carrying. But the plain fact is that although all our species are precious, the flying fox is arguably far more vital to our ecological system – and therefore to us – than the cute and cuddly koala. Don't get me wrong: koalas are beautiful, interesting, unique and also ancient inhabitants of this planet.

Humans have for thousands of years operated from the assumption that we are the supreme species and, being the most intelligent, have the unquestionable right to treat everything else, both animate and inanimate, as our resources. In exercising this assumed right, we have unfortunately allowed greed to cloud our intelligence. The consequences of this are now confronting us with massive payback.

There are prominent, reputable, independent scientists who state that we actually only have a few years left, on present trends, before the process of collapse is irreversible. Although we regard ourselves as the most intelligent species, it now seems that humans are currently set to be the only creatures to bring about their own destruction, by surrendering to a dangerous mix of greed and arrogance. Intelligence alone is not enough: it needs to be tempered by wisdom – the missing ingredient.

This chapter was written on the eve of the 2019 federal election, when neither major party paid more than lip service to the elephant in the room: climate change. On the eve of the 2022 election, this paragraph needed rewriting.

Sadly, nature is three damaging years worse off than in 2019, with neither major party showing any genuine commitment to tackling the mounting crisis. Devastation from the 2019–2020 wildfires has left people in makeshift living situations pending financial claims and now, with the pandemic that followed on its heels still impacting the country, many communities are battling homelessness and financial ruin from massive flooding.

Band-aid fixes just won't do it any more: these extreme events are nature's rebellion. We need to change our ways radically and accept that such extremes are the new norm, as the questionable cliché puts it. It's a huge waste of funds – let alone people's false hopes – to rebuild Lismore (for example) in its existing valley. We simply all need to change our priorities and behaviour, to give nature its rightful respect and supremacy.

Fortunately, not everyone has given up hope. A growing number of independent MPs attests to this. Even more, it is school students (primary, secondary and tertiary) who are taking the desperately needed initiative in changing this doomed model. Not long ago, my partner and I joined many other adults at two local rallies run by school students, one of many across Australia and part of a global student protest movement. It is our children's future we have threatened with our plundering ways and we respect their behaving in this positive way. People power, not political power! But it is not only the human species whose future is threatened.

We were drawn to Bellingen it by its perfect mix of coastline, huge rivers, high rainfall and beautiful subtropical rainforests. And, of course, the renowned buzz of the local township. We were not disappointed. In fact, the extraordinary variety of plant, animal, bird and marine life this region contains has become an irresistible stimulus for us to engage with the natural world and join with others passionate to nurture and enjoy it.

Along with this enjoyment, though, has come a growing awareness of how precious and delicate the whole ecosystem really is, and how interdependent. Like most people, I was broadly aware that our planet has already lost many species of plant and animal life as a result of human behaviour, which is largely responsible for climate change and a damaged natural world. We meet friends for coffee at our Alternatives bookshop, some of whom are experts in various branches of ecology and all of whom are seriously interested. This has turned into a learning curve for us. I began consulting environmental sites on the internet and was shocked at the huge list of species already extinct and the alarming numbers in danger of becoming so.

At one of our coffee mornings recently, I mentioned that I was researching koalas for an essay I planned to write.

'Why not bats?' a flying fox expert in the group challenged me. 'They play a much more vital role in the intricate web of nature than koalas.'

That got me thinking. I'd already embarked on my self-appointed project of writing about species at risk here. I'm writing as a lay person for lay readers, specifically those whose lives give them little or no access to the natural world – which, sadly, is too many people. I'd chosen to focus on the koala for this chapter as it's such an iconic creature and we have a current drive here to create what is referred to as the Great Koala Park on the mid-north coast, which includes Bongil Bongil National Park. This extensive forest has been a koala habitat for countless years, but extensive logging has fragmented their environment, threatening their continued survival.

A cost-benefit study is now being funded to extend and connect up the current forest areas in this region, adding a further 175,000 hectares to make a total of 315,000 hectares. It is to include major walking, cycling and horse-riding trails as well as a multi-purpose visitors' centre. We have the popularity of the koala to thank as the main drawcard for this ambitious project.

But the less feted grey-headed flying fox is also now endangered, and it plays a vital role in the preservation of a healthy ecological environment. Koalas and flying foxes both have legitimate places in our natural world, so both deserve our support and protection. Both are currently listed as needing protection. Plants, animals, birds, insects and marine life considered at risk of extinction fall into three categories: threatened, endangered and vulnerable, but all are considered to be in need of protection.

In a statement made by World Wild Life, Martin Taylor announced that, on current rates of forest clearing, the koala is on track to be extinct in NSW by 2050. So it came as a surprise to me to learn that koalas are recorded as merely vulnerable, given all the save the koala campaigns throughout Australia.

A later email from him states that warmer temperatures are sapping the moisture from gum leaves, the specific diet of koalas, leaving them dehydrated. Staff at WWL are calling for funds to continue making water feeders to set high up in gums to supplement the moisture shortage in an attempt to keep koalas alive till we achieve better logging laws and containment of climate change damage. We now have only an estimated 20,000 koalas left in NSW, and currently only about fifty thousand koalas Australia-wide, which places them in the endangered list: hence the need to support and protect them.

Like the kangaroo, the koala is a popular Australian icon worldwide, a major attraction for tourists. When Harry Windsor brought his wife Meghan on a promote-the-royals tour to Australia, women's magazines had a field day featuring shots of Meghan shrinking from cuddling a koala. No doubt she was doing her best to hide her repugnance at the bad smell they give off as a result of their diet. But, being pregnant at the time, she would certainly have been afraid of contracting the disease chlamydia.

The koala (*Phascolarctes cinereus*) is unique to Australia and some twenty million years old as a species. Contrary to popular belief, it is not a bear. Its only relative, also unique to this country, is the ground-burrowing wombat. The koala is arboreal, though, living mainly on eucalyptus leaves. Today, koalas inhabit a range of areas in Queensland, NSW, Victoria and, in smaller numbers, South Australia and even Tas-

Koala mother feeding baby.

mania, with a general preference for coastal locations. In other words, they are reasonably adaptable.

There is only one species of koala. Variations in size and colour are attributable to environmental differences: those in the northern regions tend to be smaller and lighter in colour, with silver-grey fur; those in the south have longer, thicker grey-brown fur. Though their preferred diet is eucalypt, they will tackle melaleuca and leptospermum, if necessary. The reason they sleep for up to twenty-two hours a day is because this is such a restricted, low-energy diet, though they can consume a vast quantity of leaves during this short waking period. They love coastal eucalypts, but avoid tropical rainforest vegetation.

They are not prolific breeders. One main explanation relates to this diet: it apparently affects the male libido. Koalas reach physical maturity at about eighteen months, but often don't find a mate till they are four or five years old, which restricts their reproduction rates. Breeding season in this region occurs between September and December, when they begin their bellowing to attract females. It's now known that the bellowing is what triggers ovulation in females. I once experienced this when living in South Gippsland. My attic bedroom opened directly onto the higher branches of a Nicholii gum: the bellowing that awoke me one night sounded like a cross between a motor mower starting up and a large pig. No sleep that night!

Tracking studies have discovered that each male has a unique bellow, which can tell a listening female not only the size of the male, but also caution her against inbreeding. Males also give off a terrible smell at this time – a mixture of urine and a powerful musky scent. No doubt attractive to female koalas, though – or there'd be no breeding! The males often behave aggressively towards rivals at this time; females, by contrast, become suddenly quite sociable with one another during breeding season. Otherwise, koalas are loners, and always sleep each in its own tree.

The young are born jellybean-sized and are suckled until they grow bigger and open their eyes. The average length of an adult is sixty to seventy-five centimetres, so the newborn is minute by comparison. As the baby (or cub) grows, it clings to its mother's back when she climbs.

The Australian Koala Foundation project encourages the public to

Australia's best known and most popular native.

make monthly donations and assigns a particular animal as theirs to visit in the sanctuary. Another example of koala preservation projects is that of is the 'Saving our Species Iconic Koala Project, 2017–2021' (Office of Heritage and Environment).

Human-induced climate change (droughts, bushfires, rising temperatures, erratic rainfall) has obviously impacted hugely on most of our native species. In the case of koalas, damaging factors include logging, urban and suburban developments requiring clearing, dog attacks and road deaths. The other major factor – stemming from all of these – is that their compromised immune systems have succumbed to disease, mainly chlamydia, now widespread among koala populations.

The logging problem alone is frightening. Figures supplied by World Wild Life Australia in October 2016, reveal that under new logging agreements in NSW more than 2.2 million hectares of koala habitat can be cleared, and eighty thousand of this literally bulldozed. Potential impact data has still not been provided by the NSW government, and logging is still happening at alarming rates. This destruction of forest trees in the state will put not only koalas but many other forest species in line for rapid extinction. Unless we can stop it.

A range of measures currently in place to address these issues is having mixed success; some of the problems seem almost insurmountable. Save our Species and the Rural Fire Service, for instance, are doing active work here. The former are providing seed-funding to reforest corridors between existing koala habitats, encouraging private landholders to participate, though even as they carry out this work, logging continues to clear more and more of our remaining forest areas. The RFS is working on koala fire management risk plans. Virologists and other scientists are researching and documenting disease-prone areas.

The issue of chlamydia and work to contain/eradicate it is an example of just how complex the plight of the koala has become. Culling of diseased koalas is clearly indicated as a control measure, but their popularity with the general public is so strong that, when a secret cull in Cape Otway, Victoria, was leaked to the media, there was a huge

A case of chlamydia.

outcry. Catch-22. Or, to put it another way, the sentimental desire to protect each koala, admirable as it is, actually undermines the species as a whole, because the disease is not being contained.

The current situation is mixed. In Queensland, NSW and ACT, koala numbers are down; in Victoria and South Australia, their population is effectively too high in relation to available food supply. The tree deaths that are resulting in these highly populated areas (mainly *Eucalyptus viminalis*) are affecting not only koalas but other wildlife dependent on this habitat. The secret cull in the Otway Ranges, for example, was not only to remove diseased animals from contaminating others, but also to put starving koalas out of their misery – the cruel to be kind approach.

Koalas are biologically unique, the only living representative of the marsupial family, *Phascolarctidae*. Together with our greater gliders and ringtail possums, they are also the only species to survive entirely on leaves. A koala needs roughly a hundred trees to supply its needs. Logging, urbanisation and climate change, in particular, have forced them to occupy smaller habitats, putting a strain on both them and the trees. Not to mention all the other creatures who rely on these increasingly small pockets of natural habitat. So the case of the koala is a somewhat vexed one.

Flying foxes have suffered from bad press. In fact, they are intriguing creatures and surprisingly beautiful. Now that I am getting to know them, I have become really fond and protective of them. There are four main species of what are termed megabats or fruit bats in Australia – the black, the little red, the spectacled and the grey-headed. These bats belong to the only mammal group (*chiroptera*) capable of sustained flight.

They occur in varying parts of the country, typically, though not always, near coast or water. They fly, as birds do, whereas squirrels glide. They differ from birds, though, in that birds have feathers and foxes are furred – because they are mammals. Scientists had for many years regarded them as being related to primates. They do resemble us in some ways: their eyes face the front and they have opposable thumbs, though their mating and birthing behaviour bear comparison with lemurs. And they are placental animals.

However, DNA bone analysis has resulted in their recent classification as simply bats, a separate category. They have one distinct feature that places them in a separate category: they roost with their heads facing downwards. This is evidently because, despite their having solid bones, their legs are not strong enough to support their body weight and massive wingspan. I find all this weird, but fascinating.

The grey-headed flying fox (*Pteropus poliocephalus;* GHFF) is the commonest species on the mid-north coast, but ranges widely from Adelaide to Tasmania and up as far as Rockhampton and beyond. The GHFF is presently classified as vulnerable (*Biodiversity Conservation Act, 2017*) because although they appear to be plentiful, their numbers ac-

Flying fox in flight, showing quaint 'pyjama pant'.

Flying foxes at dusk.

tually in rapid decline over a short time span: between 1990 and 2000, a sharp drop of about 30% has been estimated. It can be deceptive living here: we see so many that it's natural to assume all is well, but the truth is that as habitat availability shrinks, the flying foxes are forced to crowd into remaining habitats.

We often watch as they fly over our property at dusk in a seemingly endless stream, their strange black shapes silhouetted against the sky. Inspiring to think to that this ritual has been going on for thousands of years! Some scientists claim they go back thirty-five million years.

Seen close-up, they are appealing creatures, with faces as endearing as those of puppies. They have large, expressive eyes in foxy faces which show definite individual variation. They have light grey heads with a distinctive reddish furred collar not unlike the fox furs women used to wear, whereas the body fur is thick, dark grey. The feet and hands have long, elegant digits. The hands resemble ours, but are extraordinarily elongated, stretching to provide the framework for the huge wings they support, for all the world like the spokes of an umbrella – or that's how I see them. Some I saw this morning were stretched out in flight, and their furry legs (specific to the GHFF) looked like a pair of trousers because along one side of the leg is a smooth skin flap, held in place in a

The trousered look on full view.

squared-off fashion by a muscular join. The span of the wings gives an exaggerated impression of their size.

This morning I spent some fascinating time on Bellingen Island with a highly informed friend watching their noisy mating rituals, conducted as usual in bright sunlight. Although feeding time begins at dusk, GHFFs are obviously not strictly nocturnal. The reason feeding starts near dark is probably to reduce the risk of detection by predators (goannas, carpet pythons, powerful owls and sea eagles – though the latter find easy pickings when the young foxes are plentiful). The biggest threat, of course, is habitat damage – human-caused.

Their diet of choice is the nectar of native blossoms, though if they are in short supply, they will readily devour fruit from planted fruit trees, spitting out the fibrous membrane of the fruit to lighten their

Feeding on pollen from a grevillea.

load for flying, as I learned from the wonderful book by Vivien Jones *Flying Foxes: Australian Night Foresters*. To drink, they skim over water to wet their bellies, then land on a nearby branch to suck up the moisture. And they do, of course, consume fruit juice as they feed. GHFFs will travel up to fifty kilometres from their campsites to their feeding grounds.

Mature males usually mark out their mating territories along tree branches. One particular male with a highly distinctive mark was carefully observed over a period of eleven years to note its patterns of behaviour. It seems a male will usually move up to a higher branch each year at mating time, apparently gathering status and thereby attracting more females. Females often approach males, but make it clear when they are not interested in mating, as I have witnessed. Groupings in a camp seem to be based on seniority rather than gender. Mating takes place in daylight, as mentioned, and usually around April. The long

Mother and baby.

gestation period, lasting about twenty-seven weeks, is followed by three to four months' lactation time. For the first four or five weeks, she carries her young with her all the time; he will only be 'parked' in the camp when he is old enough to regulate his own temperature. The female will normally have one offspring each year; if twins, one will almost certainly die. Full maturity of the offspring takes about three years.

From this, it is apparent that maintaining their numbers is already difficult, without the exacerbation of climate change and habitat destruction.

A number of detrimental factors threaten the GHFF, and they all relate to impaired habitat. It occurs to me that the general prejudice against them must be a factor. They are considered diseased: they are host carriers of three zoonotic diseases (Hendra, Menangle and Lyssavirus) but actually pose little danger to humans. Hendra, for instance, can only affect humans if contracted from infected horses. Lyssavirus has only ever caused two recorded human deaths, both in Queensland. We now have a vaccine for it which can be administered safely both before and after contact.

Other factors which have caused GHFFs to be under threat all relate to human activity, virtually the same factors which have led to koalas being classified as vulnerable. An increasing cause of the decline in numbers of GHFFs is rising temperatures. They are capable of tolerating 42 to 43% before they die of heat exhaustion. For instance, where we live, during a heatwaves with temperatures reaching a maximum of forty-five degrees centigrade in 2004, researchers working on Bellingen Island estimated there were somewhere between five thousand and seven thousand fatalities.

As with koalas, forest clearing is a huge factor, causing gaping disruptions to their vital habitat and forcing them to occupy confined spaces in urban environments.

Why are they listed as being in need of protection? The GHFF plays a vital role in preserving the health and diversity of our forest trees; indeed it is becoming more important than ever as we humans destroy more and more of the remaining forests for timber to meet the demands of our increasing population. If the GHFF-preferred diet of nectar and tropical forest tree fruit is diminished and they are forced to live on introduced produce, their role of spreading indigenous pollen from their bodies and seeds in their droppings over large areas of natural habitat, covering wider territory than bees and insects are capable of, is severely restricted.

This is especially vital now with so many cleared areas between pockets of forest – the seeds they scatter over open sections help regenerate what has been lost and the combined pollination and seed dispersal activity maintain rainforest hardwood trees, native figs and palms. No other species or natural process can fill this role.

So: koalas or bats? The answer has to be: both. Both are unique. Koalas are popular drawcards for tourists as well as Australians, attracting much-needed funding for environmental conservation and restoration generally. Our GHFFs are vital to the health and survival of our native forests, and need to be in large numbers to effectively carry out the work they do. Without them, the forests would be in serious trouble, along with all the living creatures they support, including koalas. Also, because both creatures are unique, they deserve protection for this reason alone. The ecosystem is a highly interdependent one: everything needs to be in balance. Our role as humans now needs to be a restorative one, to attempt to redress that imbalance. To do this, we need to combine our superior intelligence with wisdom, to relearn how to cherish the natural world. To share our planet with all living creatures, not continue to dominate. And time is fast running out.

Spiders: Much Maligned

Did you know that spiders are among the earliest living creatures on land? I certainly didn't when I began my research! Evidence supports the claim that they date from roughly four hundred million years ago, evolving from their thick-waisted ancestors who lived in the sea.

The earliest proof is based on fossil finds such as the *Attercopus finbriungus*, which dates from three hundred and eighty million years ago, during the Devonian period. These primitive, evidently slow and cumbersome terrestrial spiders actually pre-date the dinosaur.

The early Devonian period was mild and relatively stable, with various terrestrial plant and insect life emerging, so it seems likely that the earliest arthropods began responding to these new, advantageous conditions. The broad term arthropod refers to creatures having external skeletons and jointed limbs. The word comes from Ancient Greek *arthro* (joint) and *podos* (footed) and includes scorpions, ticks, insects and centipedes.

Many people are afraid of spiders – me included. We're considered to suffer from arachnophobia. But we're fascinated, too: think *Spiderman*, for example, and stories in which spiders play a central role. I remember learning at school about Robert the Bruce, fierce warrior and briefly King of Scotland (the Pretender to English loyalists) being locked in a prison cell, where he watched a spider slowly and patiently spinning its delicate web. Legend has it that it gave him determination and patience concerning his own predicament.

The truth is, surprisingly few spiders are a real threat to humans and death from a spider bite hardly ever occurs. Many will bite if feeling threatened, causing pain and sickness to varying degrees, but these symptoms are usually short-lived, not requiring medical treatment or

Spangled spiderweb, taken by an artist friend, Carol Helman, in her garden.

hospitalisation. That being said, we need to maintain a respectful vigilance. As I write this, parts of NSW are experiencing massive flooding – the combined effect of la Niña and climate change.

Ground-dwelling spiders must abandon their homes and seek shelter in dry places, and our homes can often make perfect sanctuaries. Places like footwear, under couches and other furniture and even inside wardrobes are popular choices for some species, so these need to be checked cautiously. Numerous trapdoor and funnel-web spiders have been found in homes in Macksville (not far from us) because of the recent flooding rains. Remember, if a spider feels cornered, of course it may attack.

Spiders live almost everywhere on the planet, with the notable exception of polar regions and high mountain tops. They are obligate predators (meaning that they need to eat other creatures to stay alive). That being said, they are totally non-selective or generalist predators – even, in some species, capable of eating their own kind. Some are known to snare birds on occasion; indeed, there was a case many years go where a spider was found to have killed and feasted on a chicken. I was surprised to learn that spiders are one of the most voracious consumers of invertebrates in the earth's ecosystem: a single spider can consume up to two thousand insects a year!

This may sound like an over-dramatic claim, but in effect, without spiders, humans would struggle to feed themselves. Because a spider's diet typically includes grasshoppers, aphids, leafhoppers, beetles and caterpillars, they're the farmer's or agriculturist's friends: without spiders, the crops which supply us and the stock used to supply meat would suffer severe damage. Spiders also love mosquitoes, which many scientists claim are one of the main causes of human disease and death. Far more dangerous than those spiders we commonly regard with such dread!

The earliest spiders, the *Liphtius*, were ground-dwellers or burrowers. The funnel-web and the trapdoor spider are the main species to have changed very little over so many million years. Like their ancient forebears, they are long-livers, their females often outliving several males to produce countless spiderlings. The popular story that female spiders are bigger than their hapless partners and simply eat them once they've fulfilled their procreative purpose does have some truth – at least among many species. Our popular saying – the female of the species is more deadly than the male – clearly derives from spiders, and is hardly complimentary to either arachnid or human.

The diversity of spider species and their behavioural patterns is vast. For example, all spiders make silk, but only some of them make webs with which to trap prey, and even here there is variety: some webs are sticky, for fly-catching; some work through vibration; some are designed to catch ground-dwelling insects and others target flying insects. Funnel-web and trapdoor spiders (and others which retain some of their primitive, distinguishing features) use their burrows to trap prey. In her fascinating book titled simply *Spiders* (1976), Barbara York Main reveals in detail how these species still design, construct and operate their various silk tunnels and various web traps. The skill and complexity she describes are impressive.

As York Main details in her book, spiders use their spinning skills in a variety of different ways. While the primitive tunnel-makers use their silk as a building material for building a home-cum-nursery, others use their web to trap crawling or flying prey; yet others, especially small or young ones, create long, silk threads which they remain attached to and release, allowing the wind to take them to often quite distant places. It's called ballooning. This is certainly one of the ways in which different species have extended their original habitats over time, and very likely still do. Spider silk is surprisingly tough – in fact, it is the most flexible natural biomaterial known. The silk of the golden orb spider, for example, is strong enough to catch both birds and flying foxes. Extraordinary!

Before we move on to look at some of the main spiders found on the mid-north coast, here are some interesting facts. Spiders can live from one year to over forty. Worldwide, almost forty-five thousand species of spider have been recorded, yet there are likely to be many not yet identified.

For instance, a 2011 expedition led by experts from the California Academy of Sciences, identifies three hundred new species on Luzon Island in the Philippines, in the space of forty-two days. And earlier this year a new spider was identified not far from here, now listed as *Assa Wollumbin*. We need to protect those we know about and continue to discover more of those yet unknown because not only are they are precious and interesting; they are vital for our own sustenance.

An essay-length discussion cannot possibly encompass all Australian spider species, so I have selected some that seem to be the better known – those you're more likely to see either in gardens, sheds or bush and forest, and those you have possibly already encountered in your own home. All those included here are found along the mid-north coast, though none are confined to this region. Many will already be familiar names, too, though, as I was, you may find that you've been misinformed about them.

There are several different ways to categorise spiders, all of them valid. We have already referred to York Main's broad distinction between the Primitives (those that have changed little from their ancient forbears) and the Moderns (those which have adapted and mutated over time). Another useful way to classify them is by how they live, breed and feed themselves: broadly, the hunters (or Primitives) and the weavers and spinners, who comprise what York Main describes as the Moderns. This is a huge simplification, though.

For instance, the hunters are all ground-dwellers, yet some of these species actually build quite complicated abodes with silk linings in their tunnels, and even separate chambers for breeding and nurturing, food storage or even safety chambers in case of attack. Among the spinners and weavers, some build at ground level, while others make webs above the ground, based in each case on the habits of the prey which forms their diet.

The spinners and weavers can also be divided into those who lure their prey into webs and those who lie concealed, waiting to ambush their prey. In this chapter we will look at some of each. Because of the variety and complexity of spider genera, they will not be ordered, since categorisation is bound to oversimplify the differences.

First – for no obvious reason – the white-tailed spider *(Lampona cylindrata)*, a species with a bad reputation perhaps not really deserved, because few forms of this spider are actually dangerous to humans, though a bite can cause temporary local pain. The white-tail is a hunter and a nocturnal feeder. It is usually dark red or grey, with orange legs; females grow to about eighteen millimetres in length and males to about twelve millimetres. The female will spin several sacs into which she will lay about ninety eggs, which she will guard until they hatch.

This prolific output is needed because of the high casualty rate: only a small percentage will make it to adulthood, partly because the tiny spiderlings often seize on their siblings as their first (easiest) meal. This may come as a shock. It did to me too, though we need to see it as part of the complex biodiversity fabric. The fact that these rather small spiders also prey on and devour other spiders is an example of this interdependency at work. Like many spiders, white-tails tend to move indoors during the wetter months.

Among the best known of the hunter and ambush spider group are the wolf spider (*Trochosa ruricola*) and the huntsman (*Sparassidae* family), both found throughout Australia, though there are numerous

Wolf spider.

species of each. From those I've seen either in the flesh or in photos, they all look pretty forbidding, and like any spider feeling trapped, both will bite a human, though, of the two genera, only the wolf spider's bite may require some medical attention.

A distinguishing feature of wolf spiders is the three rows of eyes located at the front which, seen by a spotlight at night, glow green. A common, but by no means definitive, feature of a huntsman is its hairiness, especially on the legs. But given there are so many variations in each genus, they can be hard to identify. Both have many characteristics in common, retaining some vestiges of their common ancestor, so belong in the Primitive category, like the funnel-web and trapdoor.

None are web-builders, so feed by ambushing their prey and are therefore swift-moving. They differ, though, in that burrowing is rare among the huntsman and wolf species, and only ever minimal.

The breeding time for both tends to be during the warm summer months and, because they love humidity, they can often be found indoors during heavy summer rains. We recently had no less than six grey wolf spiders visit us this summer: four in the en suite, one at the foot of our bed, and one obviously ventured further, because my partner was bitten on the hand in bed, and was easily identified by its fang marks. A large red swelling appeared, which he sprayed with eucalyptus oil. Some itching occurred a couple of days later, then the swelling disappeared. Nothing to panic about! I admit to being a bit spooked by bedtime visits, though, and we're puzzled as to how they got in, since we have a well-sealed, modern home. It wasn't the same spider, we're confident, as he captured each one and placed it outside in the dense garden.

Something needs to be said about our huntsman, since he/she is such a familiar visitor, both inside and out. There are in Australia ninety-four recorded species, and obviously others not yet identified. An example is a bright orange fellow found in far-north Queensland in 2006, evidently confined to one small location. None are fatal to humans, despite their ferocious appearance – at worst, a bite might require brief medical attention – and they are not aggressive.

Huntsman spider.

The average lifespan of a huntsman is up to two years. Once breeding season dwindles around May (up here), the older ones will likely die; the others will simply hibernate through winter. Unlike many species of spider, huntsman females don't tend to devour their hapless male partner after mating. They seem to coexist quite amicably. The female will spin a silken sac into which she will lay about two hundred eggs. She will hide the sac under bark or rock, for example, and stay on guard for several weeks until they hatch. This is the one time she may be aggressive, if approached.

Not only are huntsmen quite a civilised genus: there are actually species known as social or flat huntsman who live in communes of up to three hundred, raising their offspring communally and even feeding one another. As with snakes and cicadas, for example, they need to shed their old skins as they grow. Amazingly, only yesterday we found a shiny young huntsman on the shed wall, inside, with his cast-off old skin stuck too the wall just below him.

Huntsmen are popularly referred to as backyard buddies (an American term) because they perform a useful role in pest control, both indoors and out, and are particularly fond of mosquitoes and cockroaches.

They, in turn, are food for birds, geckos, and even the egg parasites of flies and wasps.

The black house spider (*Badumna insignis*) is one you will almost certainly have encountered in your own home, because it is very widespread across Australia. It is a robust creature, though only about 1.5 centimetres in body length. Its carapace and legs are dark brown to black, with a charcoal-grey abdomen, and faint white dorsal markings.

At breeding time, the female constructs several white silk sacs which she attaches to her web retreat. She will stay with her brood until they hatch and disappear. Black house spiders mature in summer and live for roughly two years. Although their webs are usually to be found on tree trunks or logs, they are frequently found inside our homes, often in the corners of window frames. I have seen one in the shower base of our en suite twice in the last week. Before beginning my research on spiders, I would have killed it automatically; now I think differently, and knowledge is calming my fears. Admittedly, I learned that this harmless-looking little creature is poisonous (though not fatally), but it is not aggressive. So I went to bed content to leave it in the adjacent shower.

There is a related brown spider too, though it is less common and possibly imported by early settlers. This one tends to frequent cupboards and wardrobes, so we simply need to be aware.

Daddy-long-legs spiders (*Pholcus phalangioides*) are familiar to all of us. They are often indoors, usually quite high up in the corners of walls. They look so delicate and innocent with their tiny bodies (only seven to nine millimetres) and absurdly long, spindly legs that I used to love them as a child, with their loose, open webs. Surprisingly, though, this species feeds not only on insects, but on other spiders too. Dear little cannibals!

The Sydney funnel-web (*Hadronycheccerberea*) is one of many funnel web species and the one most often seen on our mid-north coast. Some funnel-web spiders can be alarmingly large: indeed, the world's largest spider is a variety of funnel-web found in the Northern Rivers region

Daddy-long-legs spider.

Sydney funnel-web spider.

of Australia. It commonly grows to the size of an adult human hand! A bite from a funnel-web is capable of killing a human child in fifteen minutes. We need to take them seriously.

As already mentioned, the funnel-web spiders are what York Main describes as Primitives –that is, spiders which have changed little over the last three hundred and eighty-odd million years. They are a terrestrial, sombre-coloured species, rather bulky for their size, and burrowers. They construct burrows as dwellings, but also for various other purposes. These burrows are typically more or less permanent. Like the other well-known Primitive, the trapdoor spiders (which we'll come to shortly), they have surprisingly intricate and sophisticated building designs and techniques that are worth looking into in more detail. First, though, some details about their living, mating and breeding behaviour.

The Sydney funnel-web is the most common one on the mid-north coast. A reasonably large creature, the female grows up to thirty-five millimetres in length; the male, to about twenty-five millimetres. The head is black, the abdomen dark brown or purple. An identifying feature is the fine hair which covers the legs and body. Dare I say unlike the human species, the male takes about four years to mature; the female longer. Once he performs his mating duty, the male usually dies within six to eight months, whereas females can breed for several more years.

Her egg sac contains hundreds of eggs which she stores in the burrow until they are hatched as independent spiders and left to their own devices. Nature has reasons for species' breeding practices. Large numbers of turtles are born because the rush of the newly hatched is hazardous: few will escape the beaks and claws waiting to snatch them as they struggle frantically to reach the relative safety of the sea. In the case of many spider species, such as the funnel-web, the large hatching-rate is to cater for the fact that fellow siblings are often the first meal! Survival of the fittest in action! The usual diet of adult funnel-webs consists of insects, though they are known to tackle both frogs and lizards several times their size. The bite of a funnel-web can be fatal to humans, but as the species is not aggressive, bites almost never happen.

Let's look now at the trapdoor spider (*Migolas rapax*), the other well-known species to have survived with almost no change since the Devonian period. Though similar in size to the funnel-web, they are less robust. Like the funnel-webs, they are not striking-looking spiders, but the male has the distinguishing feature of boxing-glove-shaped palps at

A trapdoor spider's home, showing how they build a camouflaged setting.

the front of its head. The male dies after mating (a common thing among arachnids).

The female holds her eggs in a cocoon which she guards in the burrow until they emerge as spiderlings ready to disperse. As with the funnel-webs, their prolific numbers compensate for the low survival rate. Trapdoor burrows are normally two hundred and fifty millimetres in depth and twenty-five millimetres wide, but unlike those of the funnel-web, they have a door or lid at the top. They are apparently among

Trapdoor spider.

the longest-living arachnopods, with one on record as having lived forty-three years, and then only dying as the result of a wasp sting! Though the bite of a trapdoor is not fatal to humans, it can certainly cause local pain.

Another spider which has apparently evolved from the funnel and trapdoor species, to which it is closely related is the mouse spider (*Missulena occatoria*). It is more compact, and looks quite harmless, being dark brown or black in colour, but don't be deceived: it has huge fang-sheaths at the front of its head which can deliver a highly toxic venom. No human deaths from this species are recorded in Australia, but certainly, seek medical help if bitten.

At about four years of age, the male will seek a mate; mating takes place in the female's burrow. Having performed his procreational duty, he will then die. The female mouse spider's egg sac contains roughly sixty eggs, which she will guard secretively till they hatch. Mouse spiders usually only emerge from their lidded burrows after heavy rain, which is the time for humans to be watchful. A variant of this species is the red-headed mouse spider, which differs only in the colour of its head.

Redback spider, female.

The redback spider (*Latrodectus mactans*) does not belong to the Primitives just discussed; it belongs with them only in the sense that its bite is serious for humans and that it is also endemic in Australia. Fortunately, scientists have developed antivenom for all three of these species' bites.

The redback belongs rather in the same family as the house-and cupboard spiders. It does create a web, but of a more basic, tangled and less sophisticated kind. Its web is funnel-like – a place to hide and keep vigil, with sticky silk threads dangling to the ground to trap prey. It's the female redback which bears the vivid red or orange stripe on its back, though close scrutiny can detect a faint version on the back of the (smaller) male. I haven't been close enough to verify this. What I can confirm, though, is that my partner found two (a male and a female) with a tangle of web at the bottom of our laundry cupboard under the rim when he was cleaning two days ago. Startling, considering what a modern, light and airy home ours is – no doubt tempted indoors by recent heavy rains. But it amazes me how they get in.

The female matures at two to three months, can live for two to three years, and spins between three and eight sacs, each containing up to three hundred eggs. Few of these will make it, though: siblings often turn on each other for their first meal, and wasps love them! The male's life is short and perhaps merely perfunctory, with an average lifespan of six to seven months. Redbacks favour insects and frogs by way of diet, though they are known to tackle small birds, too. This is less startling when you know that they don't so much eat large prey; they simply suck out the juices. The redback is an example of an ambusher.

Another interesting spider which conceals itself, ambush-style, is the rufous net-casting spider (*Deinospis subrufa*), which typically inhabits open woodland and garden shrubbery. A slender, long-legged creature, the female grows to twenty-five millimetres and the male from ten to fifteen. It's the ingenuity of its web-building and ambush strategies that make it so fascinating.

Each night, it builds a rectangular-shaped web which looks no bigger than a postage stamp, locating it in low vegetation where it knows prey will land. It then hangs upside-down above the web, its front two legs on each side holding the net outstretched, well-concealed, having deposited specks of white faeces close to the web. It has large eyes which

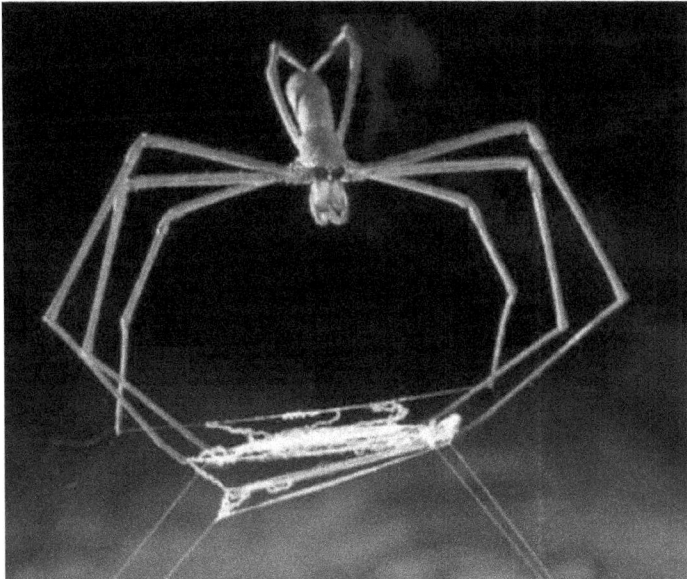

Rufous casting spider.

give it low-light vision and, the instant a hapless insect goes to check the faeces, it stretches its web to two or three times its apparent size and casts it over the trapped victim. It then quickly bites the prey, wraps it in silk thread and, even as it consumes this meal, will usually begin building the next net. This sophisticated ritual may be hard to comprehend, but we've actually observed it happen in a shrub below our deck.

In addition to the tunnel-building species (the *fossorials*) and the ambushers are the web-makers or weavers, which construct webs either at or above ground level. Some conceal themselves – say in a rolled-up leaf – and lie low ready to ambush their prey; others use their webs to trap or entangle their prey.

It's worth diverging from our brief discussion of different spider species to look at some of the extraordinary skills spiders display in their building, breeding and hunting strategies. The range is vast and complex, so I'll have to try and keep it brief. Anyone interested can find any number of more detailed studies, though I've found Barbara York Main's book – published many years ago – hard to beat. She delves into the details of the various ways spiders build according to their needs and habitats. For example, trapdoor spiders are so-called because they are not just capable of digging neat tunnels which end in perfectly circular openings at ground level; they also construct hinged doors which open and close, and fit rather like bath plugs complete with finely bevelled edges – secure from attack and largely waterproof.

These burrows, sometimes even lined with spun silk, are permanent homes not only from which to ambush passing prey, but also often replete with mating chambers and nesting chambers or nurseries, each with separate doors. To build these burrows, they use mud and saliva-juices to create smooth, pottery-like plaster walls. Another solution to the external door is a cover made of spun silk. This one appears to operate simply by the spider drawing a gathering thread to open or close it.

The earliest cobwebs seen by settlers in Australia tended to be at or close to ground level. Spiders which live at or above ground level and build webs are known as orb-weavers (*Araneidae*). The only kind of web we tend to see at ground level are the tiny webs you find scattered across grassy areas after heavy dew or rain. Being in a subtropical, summer rainfall climate here, we see lots. Apparently they're made by mini-spiders which are quite harmless to humans. Look closely, though, and be amazed at how delicately they're built.

Only three other kinds of orb-weavers will be looked at here: the St Andrews Cross, the garden orb-weaver and the golden orb-weaver. The St Andrews Cross spider is largely confined to the eastern coast of Australia, especially here on the mid-north coast; the others are found more widely, and you may well have seen them. Like them, they use sticky thread to entrap their prey, but they have what I think is a unique strategy for hauling them in – a draw-thread which, when they tighten it, has the effect of lifting their victim off the ground, rendering it helpless.

At one to one and a half centimetres in length (the female; the larger one), the St Andrew's Cross spider is of average arachnid size. The female is the attractive one: decorating the creamy-coloured body, she has distinct horizontal bands in red, yellow and black. The male is not just smaller, but plainer, being an overall creamy colour. The young spider, also this creamy colour, quickly establishes itself by building its own *stabilimentum* (stable web structure).

The *stabilimentum* of the juvenile spider is is a perfect circle, rather like a doily, in which they conceal themselves to both catch prey for themselves and hide from the risk of becoming prey. It is thought that this web also provides some sunshade. The female is the adult web-spinner. She builds an intriguing structure based on a diagonal cross-shape (hence the name). The substance of this strong *stabilimentum* consists of ribbon-like zigzag threads woven in blue and white silk to reflect the UV rays, thereby attracting flying insects in search of nearby flowers.

Once the prey is thus trapped into the sticky web, the spider hastily spins a thread around it to immobilise it. The skill and precision with which the St Andrew's Cross is executed is astounding.

St Andrews spider.

Mating occurs in summer to autumn. As in many species, arguably including our own, the males are obliged to compete. Several males – some of them showing injuries inflicted by other females who attacked them when they failed to impress – will line up around the periphery of her web, hoping to be chosen. This attractive and interesting spider is not harmful to humans. We had one nest across a garage window a couple of years ago, and watched hundreds of spiderlings scuttle off at hatching, knowing few would survive. We were sad to see her gone one morning.

Garden orb-weaver spider.

There are over a hundred species of garden orb-weavers. One of the common ones, which we have in our part of the world, is the *Eriophora* – a stout creature of one to two and a half centimetres (larger being female). It is usually reddish-brown or grey in colour and has a roughly triangular-shaped abdomen covered in an attractive leaf pattern, and hairy legs. It's the web-building of this spider that I find especially interesting. The web typically spans two metres, an elegant, wheel-shaped structure, strong and vertically geometric. This in itself is impressive, but even more so is the fact that this massive edifice is built each evening for the night's catch, then dismantled at dawn – a diurnal ritual and a massive workload, surely! Its lifespan is short: only about twelve months from maturity. The female will lay her eggs in fluffy cocoons in summer-autumn, then die the following year.

Golden orb-weaver spider.

Lastly, the golden orb-weaver (*Nephilidae*). Again, there are many variations and their habitat ranges from dry woodland and scrub to sand dune and mangrove coastal areas. Our main local specimen is quite large: the female, two to four centimetres; and the male, roughly five centimetres – a reversal of the more common trend. They are usually a golden-brown colour with yellow and reddish-orange banded legs, though they can be paler. Their unique feature, I think, is their webs, which are made of sticky, spun golden silk, large, strong and semi-permanent, unlike the web of the hard-working garden orb-weaver. Their prey can range from insects to butterflies and cicadas, and can even stretch to consume the odd flying fox! I've seen a photo of one such case. Like its garden cousin, it follows the practice of binding its prey in silk to render it helpless.

I could go on and on. Spiders have proved to be a fascinating subject, but I'm conscious of the need to keep this book at a strictly non-scientific, condensed level. I'd like to end this discussion by briefly considering two things: why spiders matter to us and our planet and what are the behaviours and conditions which are threatening their healthy survival.

Spiders matter because they are such skilled and resourceful creatures. Some of their web and tunnel designs show a level of sophisticated materials use, capacity to adapt to a given habitat and to problem-solve in ways that make me, at least, want to question the idea of intelligence. We can learn from them – as Robert the Bruce did in prison long ago. They serve a vital role in controlling populations of insects like grasshoppers and other pests that attack farmers' crops (better than using pesticides, as we now clearly know).

Their silk thread is remarkably strong, as mentioned earlier, and is being used already in some surgical situations. It's worth just mentioning here that a human cloak was once made entirely of spider silk. I can't give you details – it was something I once read. The venom of some spiders is being used to help control some human diseases, and recently as an ingredient in certain painkillers. There are other reasons, too.

So what are the main things impacting the secure future of our arachnid populations? An obvious one, as I've admitted to personally, is arachnophobia. For me, learning more about them has largely eliminated my fear, and I'm hopeful it will for you too, if you suffer from it. Related to this phobia, and a direct result of it, is the custom to automatically kill spiders on sight. I understand the desire not to have potentially dangerous spiders indoors – I share that! But I recall my gentle grandmother whose home I lived in as a small child carefully lifting a huntsman from my bed and placing it in a shrub in the garden. There's a lesson in that, maybe. The large-scale use of chemical sprays is a huge problem – fortunately one we're starting to deal with as the message gets through. Habitat loss is another big problem affecting the fate of our precious arachnids. And climate change, obviously.

Every one of us has the capacity to modify our behaviour regarding the plight of spiders. And perhaps the best way to become motivated is to learn about them, to look for them in the world around us and respect them for their antiquity and fascinating, secretive ways of living. Like all of the creatures now under varying degrees of threat as a result of human behaviour, they deserve our respect.

Birds: Not Just Beautiful

This may come as a surprise, but it's a simple fact: humans need birds far more than they need us. Here's an interesting example. You've heard the cliché, dead as a dodo. When the dodo did finally become extinct, it was noticed that the tree species whose flower had been their staple diet had stopped propagating. Apparently, it required the droppings of the dodo to make these seeds viable: hence that tree also was doomed. Symbiosis, or interdependence: a process at the core of nature's ecosystem on which we all depend.

During my research for this chapter about bird species at risk on our mid-north coast, I discovered some interesting, but shocking, facts about our bird species. It has been estimated that since the year 1600 and until relatively recently (I was unable to get the closing date, but the implication is that it was probably early in the twentieth century), a hundred bird species are known to have vanished for human-caused reasons such as being hunted for sport and meat, traded in feathers, or captured for the pet industry.

Currently we have 828 known species in Australia, though about 12% of these are listed as vulnerable, threatened or endangered. The rate of disappearance has been embarrassingly high since European colonisation, and it's already too late to save some of those we still have from extinction, because of some already irreversible trends. But others of our unique species can still be rescued if we act now.

This chapter will look at some of those currently at risk, some of the actions that are being taken to preserve them, and suggestions about some of the ways you and I can help is this vital work

Birds are fascinating and remarkable creatures, each species having its own distinctive beauty. What is less commonly known is that they are often far smarter than we assume and display often quite complex behaviours. Indeed, as I learned from an absorbing recent publication by Professor Gisela Kaplan, *Bird Bonds* (2019), close observation reveals that they are capable of emotions (even empathy, in some species, and not always confined to their own kind) as well as forming social relationships. Professor Kaplan shows that they not only frequently form lasting pair-bonds, like humans, but that these are not necessarily linked to reproduction – simply deep attachments. Indeed, it seems that birds and humans, and a few other animal species, are the only living creatures to form close pair bonds.

Some birds are capable of imitating human speech; some are capable of forming attachments to humans whom they learn to trust. As I write this, we have a beautiful crimson rosella who sometimes sits on our balcony rail and calmly eyeballs me barely two metres away, and I know there's a positive non-verbal communication going on. It's come as a pleasant surprise for me to discover we have far more in common with birds than I'd imagined. Quite apart from their natural, varied, often colourful beauty, they have complex means of communication, and some are highly intelligent. Their vocalisations (songs), courtship rituals and adoption of striking breeding plumage, for example, or the various protective behaviours and the role-sharing parent birds engage in are fascinating. We are instinctively drawn to birds: perhaps, unconsciously, this is why.

As for their importance for humans and the whole ecosystem, each species of bird plays one or more roles in maintaining a healthy biodiversity balance. One obvious avian role is that of seed dispersal: bird droppings are scattered over the areas they inhabit and travel through; thus the natural world is vitalised through this revegetation process. Because their droppings are rich in nutrients, they also effectively contribute to the making of fertile soils.

The obvious example you'll probably think of here is chook poo, which forms the basis of fertilisers like Dynamic Lifter, but the process, in a more dispersed form, happens all through the natural world wherever there are birds. The same is true of marine habitats as well, such as

Female satin bowerbird in bower.

the way in which bird droppings help keep our precious coral reefs alive. Another example of symbiosis: seabirds and waders rely on plants and small marine life creatures for their survival, and they in turn provide essential fertilisation for the various marine ecosystems.

Like all living creatures at sea or on land, birds are important in maintaining a stable balance between prey and predator. In addition to their roles in plant propagation as pollinators and seed-spreaders, birds – like all living creatures both at sea and on land – play an important role in preserving ecosystem balance. The depletion in numbers, and especially where there is actual extinction, of a single bird species, has ripple effects within the whole biodiversity fabric.

Left to itself without human intervention, little or nothing is wasted in nature. For instance, even in death, each bird will become food for scavengers. For their part, scavenger birds such as vultures act as a clean-up crew, rapidly disposing of the carcasses of dead creatures before diseases can spread, as they themselves are immune. Perhaps this sounds a bit bizarre? Here's an example: after vulture numbers dropped in parts of Asia, it was noticed that the incidence of rabies in wild dogs increased markedly – a disease, as you know, that is transmissible to humans.

Birds play a transformative role in storing carbon, especially in forests, with positive effects that can extend as far away as a hundred kilometres. In salt marshes bordering the littoral coastline, birds such as oystercatchers, curlews and plovers keep potentially damaging insect numbers in check. It's all about balance, so it matters very much that these wader species on our mid-north coastline are all under threat to varying degrees, largely as a result of human activity.

The details of damage caused by humans vary: these will be discussed in relation to individual bird species in this region. Suffice to say here that our planet is home to roughly ten thousand species of bird and that for the past three hundred years or so our behaviour has disrupted their habitats and placed them in increasing danger, and ourselves along with them. Many of us seem unaware of this fact.

If you ask most people how they feel about birds, they are likely to say that some are very beautiful, especially the colourful species, and that they're really quite interesting. Bird calls don't generally seem to be favoured as highly as appearance in people's consciousness apart from those of kookaburras and magpies, of course – Aussie icons, like the koala and the kangaroo! Yet birds have a profound and positive influence on our moods.

My partner and I became particularly aware of this during a walking trip in France more than ten years ago. Whole days would pass without our hearing a single bird call. Friends returned from Germany have reported hearing and seeing almost no birds the whole time they were travelling about the country. Like us in France, they felt the eerie silence like a kind of grief. With the combination of rapidly increasing climate change exacerbated by continued forest clearance, we face an increasingly silent natural world as bird numbers decline.

In an ABC podcast on the mid-north coast (11 December 2020), Professor Kaplan was interviewed by local journalists on the topic of bird vocalisation in relation to climate change. It seems the shrinking numbers of bird species is not the only worry, though it is naturally the most serious. Like us, birds have trouble coping with extreme heat, vary-

Endangered crested shrike thrush.

ing from species to species. Heat stress causes them to lose energy, so they tend not to vocalise, and seek shady retreats. In the case of a heat-wave lasting several days, this can prevent them from feeding as well. Australian birds are normally adapted to coping with hot summers, but rising temperatures are increasingly challenging their capacity to adapt.

Take magpies, on which Kaplan is a renowned authority. At 27C, they tend to stop feeding in order to conserve their energy; at 35–40C, they are unable to feed, digest or vocalise. When there are several days of such heat, they become seriously at risk and some simply die. This trend will obviously become worse as temperatures continue to rise.

Before moving on to look at certain selected bird species at risk on the mid-north coast, it's worth mentioning how deep-seated is our fascination with birds. Birds feature in the ancient art of Egypt, for instance, and as drawings by Leonardo da Vinci exemplify, have even

Osprey eating fish.

inspired humans to fly. Our connection with these fellow creatures runs deep. We simply must nurture them as they increasingly suffer the devastating results of too many years of our extractive approach to nature. Yet even while there is the shameful smuggling trade in birds and the sport of shooting them, a growing number of people have taken up birdwatching because they are simply fascinated by them and in awe of their beauty and variety. This is really encouraging.

Certain bird species have had to be selected here, as the impact of climate change along with the 2019–20 extreme wildfires, followed by unprecedented flooding events, have affected far too many to include in the scope of this chapter. I have tried to select from a broad range, but am hoping you will be tempted to look further after reading this, to learn some disturbing realities, but also some positive strategies being undertaken and ways in which you too can become involved in the rescue effort.

Here are just a couple of statistics recorded since the 2019–20 fires: 54% of powerful owls, and 48% of masked owls were destroyed in the burnt forests. As for the rufous scrub bird, already listed as vulnerable before the fires, their deaths totalled 75% in the burnt areas in our region, and 47% even in the unburnt sections. It seems likely this bird may now be extinct, though we won't know until and unless someone sights one and reports it. One of the many vigil roles for citizen scientists like you and me!

Among the wader birds, one I particularly like is the beach stone-curlew (*Esacus magnnirostruos*), sadly now listed as critically endangered

Beach stone-curlew.

on the mid-north coast. We sighted one when walking along the coast in Urunga some months back, and a friend recently spotted one near the footbridge at the Valla Beach Reserve. It may have been the same bird, though the good news is that there's apparently a breeding pair in the area. We can only hope that they are able to rear their young without them falling victim to one of the many potential hazards. Although the beach stone-curlew is found more plentifully in other parts of coastal Australia, there are now only thirteen breeding pairs left in our region, so every breeding event matters.

The beach stone-curlew is quite large and thickset. Grey-brown in colour, it has yellow eyes set in a black and white patterned face, and a brown and white stripe on its forewing. It is a secretive bird usually seen alone, but occasionally in pairs, and semi-nocturnal, stalking its prey like a heron, but moving swiftly at the critical moment. The stone curlew's preferred habitats are in the littoral forests in intertidal zones near sea and tidal estuaries. It especially likes mangroves. Given that its habitats include both land and water, it enjoys a varied diet of crabs and other invertebrates, frogs, snakes and mice.

Like most waders, stone-curlews nest on the ground, just above the tideline, normally laying just one egg – though the female will lay another if the first one fails to hatch and reach maturity at seven to twelve months. All this makes them very vulnerable.

Like most waders, their eggs and chicks are exposed to the marauding of foxes, native predators or dogs off-lead. Further threats occur from damage to dunes. There are several risk factors here: vehicles invading both dune and beach, increasing erosion resulting from more extreme weather events, not to mention the damage caused by coastal development as the human population grows. The fact that bush stone-curlew numbers are not diminishing like their coastal cousins is probably mainly because they face fewer such threats. Important work to preserve the now critically endangered beach stone-curlew is being conducted by Save our Species through their Biodiversity Conservation Programme (under the *Biodiversity Conservation Act, 2016*).

Pied oystercatchers.

Another wader definitely recorded as endangered in our mid-north coast region since 2019 is the handsome pied oystercatcher (*haematopis longirostris*). They are exposed to the same sorts of threats as the beach stone-curlew. Their rudimentary nests, made of sand, shells, seaweed and three to four small eggs in a clutch, sometimes repeating the cycle where the first one fails, which it often does. Apart from the disturbance to their lives from habitat loss, they are prey to both European foxes and domestic dogs off-lead invading and marauding their breeding sites.

Of the approximately ten thousand surviving pied oystercatchers nationally, now only about two hundred and fifty of them are found on the mid-north coast of NSW. So reading that in 2019 many eggs and at least one chick were destroyed by unrestrained dogs was sad.

The September/October school holidays tend to be their most vulnerable period, because this coincides with the birds' breeding time. We

Sooty oystercatcher.

need to be made more aware of our responsibility towards these fellow inhabitants, who play an important role in the ecological fabric and whose lives are so easily destroyed by thoughtless human behaviour. Pied oystercatchers usually mate for life and share their parental roles cooperatively.

A close relative of the pied oystercatcher is the sooty oystercatcher (*Haematopus fuliginosis*), which typically lives and breeds on rocky headlands and on offshore islands. Like its near cousins, it is not confined to the mid-north coast, but was already listed as vulnerable here as early as 2000. Although I've been unable to track down a recent statistic, it is safe to assume its numbers will be significantly lower by now. Although we have occasionally sighted both sooty and pied oystercatchers on our coastal walks, we've never been close enough to hear their loud, piping calls. They seem quite shy of humans – perhaps for good reason.

The fundamental differences between waders or shorebirds and seabirds are worth noting. Waders can be found on many coastal locations throughout the world, with the exception of Antarctica, for obvious reasons. Waders often have long skinny legs to help them balance in moving water, with long necks and bills to help them catch their prey. Nature's design-for-purpose is brilliant. Take as an example the oystercatcher's bill, which ends in a distinctive triangular shape providing the functions of both chisel and knife. Their colours, too, are mostly muted greys, whites and browns for camouflage purposes. Although most waders are highly sociable, they are quite the opposite when hunting in the shallow waters, behaving competitively.

Seabirds are mostly larger, with webbed feet to help give them traction for take-off and landing. An obvious exception is the flightless penguin. Seabirds spend most of their time at sea, only checking into coastal areas long enough to breed and raise their young till fledging-stage, which is generally achieved quite quickly. Seabirds are more densely feathered than waders to make them more waterproof. The magnificent albatross is a well-known seabird, but not found in our parts; among the seabirds we see are gannets, cormorants, terns and sometimes shearwaters.

We can't move on from waders and seabirds without including the bar-tailed godwit (*Limosa lapponica*). Like most waders, they are migratory and highly sociable – except when stalking prey in the shallows and

Bar-tailed godwits.

mudflats. An almost inconceivable number of eight million of them are estimated to fly between Australia and the Yellow Sea, China, where they rest and feed before flying on to East Siberia and Alaska. Bar-tailed godwits evidently hold the time and distance record for migratory flights: one tagged bird was found to have travelled eleven thousand seven hundred kilometres from Alaska to New Zealand in just eight days on its non-stop return flight. Given their size is only thirty-seven to forty-one centimetres from tip of bill to tail-tip, this is simply remarkable.

Their colours are subdued, like those of most waders: mottled brown tones on the upper body and wing, and a more even buff below, so they are inconspicuous when feeding. Although they have long legs, they need to feed only at fairly low tide times in mudflats and sandbanks. It's their very specific dietary needs which drive them to migrate at set times. We see them from August, when their food supplies here are at their best.

Only two days ago, we were lucky enough to see three godwits from the footbridge at a nearby estuary, energetically searching for food on the sandbank below. We watched them run elegantly on their spindly legs, then plunge their long, slender bills deep into the sand when they sensed promising activity below the surface. How they can tell is a mystery. As we watched, not one but two of them came up with something – not a sandworm, but probably a small crustacean. They both scuttled to the water to wash it free of sand before swallowing it. This seems like a pretty smart tactic, a kind of food preparation. It prompts the notion that we almost certainly underestimate the skills and cognitive abilities of such small creatures. It was hard not to identify with their actions.

Migratory waders fatten up here in readiness for their long flight north to the coasts of Alaska and Siberia, where they go to breed. This journey is timed for the northern spring when the mudflats in China (for example) are teeming with mosquitoes. Reading about the numbers of godwits which engage in these marathon flights en masse, I was surprised and saddened to find that their numbers are actually declining: they are now listed as vulnerable or near-threatened. The reason, as so often, is human-induced: our development (and its consequent habitat loss) disturbs their feeding and breeding grounds in Australia and New Zealand as well as the northern countries to which they travel.

This has been clearly shown in, for example, China, near the Yellow River, where developers have built huge sea walls and reclaimed large portions of their mudflat feeding grounds to be used for industrial development. Research in 2019 found that their near cousin, the black-tailed godwit (*Limosa limosa*) is also now classified as vulnerable.

I'd like to include one other shore bird before we move on: the little tern (*Sterna limosa*) These little birds – a mere twenty-five centimetres long – are partly migratory, flying between east Asia and the mid to north coast of Australia, arriving here between September and November to breed. They are appealing creatures with their sleek, elongated soft grey upper bodies and white underbellies, set off with black head and forked tail and outer wing edges.

Little tern in flight.

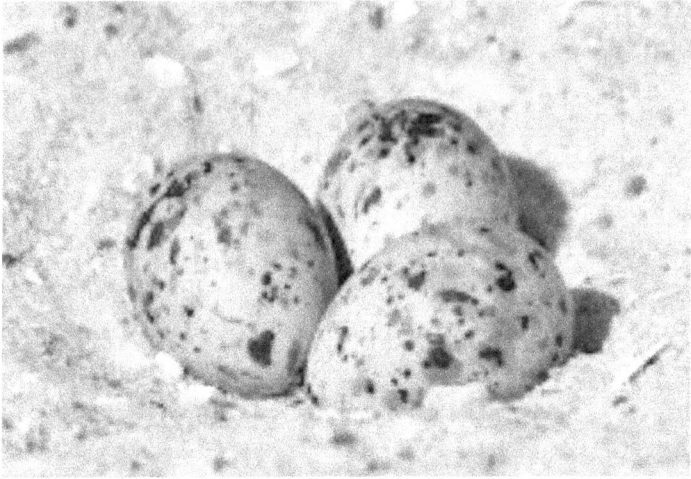
Little tern's eggs, laid vulnerably in the sand.

Being so small, and because they are among the waders to breed here, little terns are especially at risk. During breeding time, their tiny, minimal nests are readily raided by foxes and domestic dogs; like other waders which breed here, they are most at risk during September/October school holidays, as the numbers of their casualties which occur at this time clearly suggest. It's hardly a surprise to learn that they are rated as endangered on the mid-north coast. As with all our endangered or threatened species, the NSW State Recovery Plan is doing what it can, and there is plenty of scope for volunteer assistance.

Turning our attention now to the birds of the littoral forest and the coastal hinterlands of this region, where we are endowed with an enormous numbers of interesting, beautiful and often brightly-coloured bird species, we are witnessing rapidly declining numbers among almost all species. Again and again, we are faced with the ugly truth: most of the damage is human-caused. Those I've selected here should give you some idea of the uniqueness and beauty of our avian fellow-creatures and how tragic it is to lose them. There have already been too many extinctions in recent times, and the trend is accelerating. There are many ways in which we can still help; the first, it seems to me, is to learn about their plight. To know is to care.

Coxens fig-bird.

The mid-north coast has a broad range of bird species, but the numbers are too often in decline: some listed as vulnerable, some threatened, some critically endangered. Among them is the Coxen's fig-bird (*Cyclopsittadiophthalma coxmi*), the most at risk in our region, which was already listed as 'critically endangered' in 2019, before the extreme fire event.

The fig-bird is a boldly coloured, compact bird, not unlike a small lorikeet such as the scaly and rainbow species. It's by nature elusive, even cryptic; this is being compounded by the impacts of climate change and related human behaviour, making it unlikely to be seen, especially since the wildfires. Estimates in 2019 found that there were fewer than two hundred left, spread over five small populations from the forests of north coast NSW to well up into those of Queensland. The combined impacts of bushfire and human actions such as logging, clearing and residential development explain the tragic threat of extinction these beautiful birds now face.

The Office of Environment and Heritage (OEH) is doing all it can to preserve this small bird – to help it hold its place in the delicate ecosystem. Logging activity is essentially profit-driven, and pays only lip service, at best, to nurturing our wildlife. Hence there are huge cleared areas fragmenting and destroying the habitats of its precious inhabitants. No wonder the Coxen's fig-bird has fared especially badly. Because its preferred diet is fruit from the native fig tree.

OEH is supervising the planting of fig trees on farms and attempting to reforest corridors linking the remaining stands of forest, including the eucalypt stands which abut the rainforested parts. Lichen, nectar and grubs also play a part in the fig-tree bird's diet, so reforesting will encompass this too. Members of the public are encouraged to contact OEH if they are lucky enough to see one of these little birds.

Another bird now critically endangered here and elsewhere along the east coast and hinterland is the swift parrot (*Lathamus discolor*), which breeds in Tasmania and migrates to the mainland during autumn. A curious case was reported in July 2020: a single, very thin swift parrot turned up in a chook-house on Lord Howe Island, six hundred kilometres off course. It was rescued and nurtured at the Taronga Wildlife Hospital in Sydney, then released on the mid-north coast,

Swift parrot.

where it is hoped there is a small population. They nicknamed it 'Houdini'!

Swift parrots favour eucalypts such as bloodwoods and spotted gums, as well as coastal grey box and paperbarks. They are colourful birds somewhat resembling rainbow and musk lorikeets, but distinguished by their red underwings and red-purple tail. Although one or two are sometimes sighted feeding on flowering gums in the Bongil Bongil National Park near Coffs Harbour, the combined effects of bushfire and forest clearing in this richly timbered environment are seriously jeopardising its future here.

The regent honeyeater is another of our birds in this region now considered critically endangered. Until 2010, this bird was listed under the genus *Xanthomya Phrygia*; its ornithological name is now *Anthorchaera*, which makes it a member of the wattlebird species. It and the swift parrot are now estimated to be the most at risk of of extinction of

Regent honeyeater.

Australia's birds: in 2018, there were found to be only about four hundred regent honeyeaters Australia-wide, and it is already extinct in SA and western Victoria, with very rare sightings near parts of the NSW coastline.

Like the swift parrot, the regent honeyeater typically inhabited hinterland environments, but the experts believe lower rainfall there has reduced the nectar flow of the forest trees they relied on, forcing them to drift to the higher-rainfall coastal habitats. It would be tragic to lose them. They are strikingly beautiful birds: medium-sized, with a black head and throat, and exquisite markings of yellow and black, a sturdy, curved beak, with a creamy-pink line around the eye. Though quieter during breeding time, they otherwise make a soft, metallic-sounding bell-like call. It's known now that they are nomadic, often flying hundreds of kilometres in search of food now, as tagging has demonstrated.

Their desperate plight has been brought about by drier seasons and activities such as mining, timber-clearing, agricultural and residential development, and inappropriate forest management. Not all the perils they face are human-caused, of course: predators among our native fauna are known to attack their eggs and nests, and they have to compete also with aggressive native birds, including noisy miners, noisy friarbirds and red wattlebirds, but this behaviour is part of the natural ecosystem. It's the introduced species which disrupt the balance.

Positive efforts are being made to save them, with attempts to breed up their numbers in captive habitats with a view to releasing them back into the wild in time, but the huge obstacle, always, is 'where to?' when their natural environments are increasingly destroyed and reduced. We must be grateful to all those who devote their expertise (whether professionally or voluntarily) to this vital conservation work.

Owls in most of Australia are not currently among the most threatened, though there is every reason to think that this will change as their habitats and food sources shrink. The species that is already listed as vulnerable in the mid-north coast is the powerful owl (*Ninex strenua*), the largest of our Australian owls.

Powerful owl.

Classified as a hawk-owl, it stands up to sixty centimetres tall, with a wingspan that can reach a hundred and forty centimetres, and it can weigh between 1.45 and 2.2 kilograms. Powerful owls are dark grey-brown on the upper parts and whitish underneath, with dark eye-patches. They have large yellow eyes, but no facial disc, unlike some other owls. Their call is a deep, slow, resonant double hoot, the female's being slightly higher-pitched and more inflected.

The preferred habitats for powerful owls are either open woodland and sclerophyll habitats, or else wet rainforests. The mid-north coastal region is perfect for them, given that their prey consists of such medium-sized arboreal marsupials as sugar gliders, ringtail possums and flying foxes, all of which are typically plentiful here.

These magnificent birds are excellent parents who form loyal partnerships and tend to stay in the same territory (somewhere between four hundred and four thousand hectares). Their nests are usually built in the hollows of old eucalypts – usually at least a hundred and fifty years old – located in groves to protect them from other predators who might maraud their nests and steal their eggs. Two eggs are normally laid in late summer or early autumn, which are guarded by the males.

Given all this, it is easy to see why their numbers are now in decline. Apart from the predation of their eggs and young by foxes, cats and dogs – all of which are introduced – their major threats all relate to logging, which fragments their forest habitat, often destroying the old-growth trees which provide their nesting hollows, and reducing the numbers of the creatures which form their specific diet. It's a loss all round, of course. The fact that forestry industries often inappropriately harvest old-growth forests means that the powerful owls are robbed of their nest-sites. It can hardly be argued that the trees that are felled are being replaced: these powerful owls can't exactly sit around waiting at least a hundred and fifty years till the replacement trees are big enough to have developed the huge nesting hollows they require!

The same kind of problem affects virtually all our fauna when it comes to logging. Unfortunately, even fire-hazard reductions, considered necessary now with climate change and more frequent and extreme bushfires, tend both to reduce their prey and disturb their natural environment. Powerful owls don't do well when disturbed. Nor do most of us! The recently renamed Threatened Species Conservation Act goes some way towards protecting their future as a species, but the powerful owl, like all our endangered species, will benefit from all the help we can offer in speaking out against destructive, insensitive forestry practices.

The splendid yellow-tailed black cockatoo (*Calyptorhynchus funereus*) is another of our fellow creatures whose numbers are now in decline on the mid-north coast. There are five black cockatoo species in Australia, of the genus *Calyptorhynchus*, but it's the yellow-tailed black which is such a welcome presence in our part of the world. Although this name derives from that given it by George Shaw (1794) – the *Psittacus funereus* – this gloomy association is not shared by our First People, for whom it is connected with positive energy and strength. For them, all black cockatoos are associated with the power of spirit and life, bringing contentment.

Where we live, close to the coast, we have enjoyed a noisy flyover at twilight as they gather in large numbers to gossip and feed their young, giving us the impression that their numbers are flourishing. Now they have moved on to where the nuts, seeds and other tucker are more plentiful, and we miss them. Hopefully, they'll be back around here when their favoured trees are next in flower, and grub-rich. But we now realise that their numbers are actually not really plentiful at all.

Yellow-tailed black cockatoos have been declining in SA and Victoria for some years, and since 2018, a sharp decline has been noted in NSW, including this coastal region. We can't let this continue. Significant changes need to happen in our behaviour, and now, if the process is to be checked in time.

These birds are not small: at fifty-five to sixty-five centimetres in length and weighing about seven hundred and fifty to nine hundred grams, they are high-flyers whose deep, mournful cry and slow, majestic wing-flapping has something eerie and haunting about it that evokes more ancient times. I think I understand what they mean for Indigenous people. They are diurnal creatures, living on seeds, grubs and nectar, and mostly cling to the higher branches of trees, only tempted down by water or else fallen nuts or the cones from native pines, casuarinas

Yellow-tailed black cockatoo.

and banksias. Normally seen flying in pairs, dusk is their sociable time, when they are very noisy. At night or during bad weather, they seek shelter in the foliage of tall eucalypts.

Because they are usually people-shy, we rarely see that their black plumage and wing feathers are tipped with yellow; we tend only to see the yellow tail and yellow cheek patches (females). Certainly we hear them before we see them. I did see one at close range when walking in the nearby forest recently, hiding in a densely foliaged banksia at eye level, and I only saw it because I heard the crunching of banksia cones, which stopped the second I looked at it. But it made me feel privileged.

Breeding on the mid-north coast takes place between January and May. It begins with a charming ritual. The male puffs his crest and fans his tail feathers and, if acceptable, the female will then bow three or four times to acknowledge this. A suitable site is then chosen – a wide hollow in a large eucalypt – and both parents work together to line it with woodchips.

Only the female will incubate, and usually only one chick will survive, being kept with the parents until it is about six months old. This is as nature designed things, with evolutionary adaptation playing its very gradual part. But thanks to human behaviour, this natural order is now increasingly under threat. It's the same story with the yellow-tailed black cockatoos as with all our precious fauna, habitat destruction being the chief offender. We were excited by the flyovers we experienced here each twilight, believing it was proof their numbers were plentiful. The sad reality is that as more and more of their habitat is destroyed, removing the large old-growth trees they need for nesting and food supply, they are forced into smaller and smaller available forested habitat, even into built-up townships environments.

If you happen to live in a township or suburb and you notice there seem to be plenty of birds, cherish them, learn about their dietary, breeding and habitat requirements and do all you can to respond. Obviously old-growth forest trees will not usually be available in a suburban garden, but in local parks you may be luckier.

Do all you can to make sure they remain, and are not sacrificed to short-term profit-making ventures. Create native gardens around your home, if you can, to attract wildlife. We have, and the results start happening quite quickly. Teach your children about nature, take them into native forests, buy them books and visual material about our native fauna; help them to understand that humans are really part of nature, that these are our fellow creatures, whom we want to love and protect. Write protest letters to newspapers about climate change issues like coal-mining and logging. And donate to any of the many conservation organisations dedicated to saving our threatened species.

There isn't enough space here to discuss all our at-risk avian friends, but of course they are all in this category to a greater or lesser extent. Species loss has been going on at a natural rate for thousands of years: it's the speed of it now that is so alarming for us all. Birds are not only beautiful, varied and fascinating creatures – they are essential to the survival of life on this planet. To repeat: we need them more than they need us. And not only that: to know them is to love them.

Diamond Pythons

Recently we were sitting in our sunny, north-facing courtyard having breakfast and, as my partner was carrying out our green tea, he said in a quiet, measured voice, 'Don't get a fright, but turn your head slowly to the left. We have an unexpected visitor.'

We were mesmerised, more in wonder than fear. The creature was huge. Neither of us could identify it, though we guessed it had to be some kind of python. My partner looked it up on his phone and, yes, it was a diamond python (*Morelia spilota spilota*), indigenous to this area of coastal hinterland which stretches from East Gippsland near the NSW border and right up to Queensland. Neither of us had ever seen a diamond python up close, let alone in the wild.

Stretched out against the wall of the house, not a metre from where we were sitting, our visitor was all of two metres long, with a large lump in its body about halfway along. It took no notice of us, so we were able to study it at leisure. It was simply magnificent, with an intricate design in gold-ochre all over its dark brown body, branching from the diamond-shaped pattern on its head. The effect was like that of an exquisite skin tattoo.

Close-up of a diamond python showing the stunning beauty of its markings.

Snakes, I discovered, are an ancient life form. Fossil records prove that they began evolving during the Cretaceous period, over a hundred and thirty million years ago. There is also evidence that snakes and birds once had a shared lineage. The cloacal spurs in front of where the body and tail connect in snakes such as boas and pythons are thought to be remnants of legged reptiles from an earlier evolutionary stage. Their antiquity is awe-inspiring; compared to them, we humans are mere upstarts. This alone makes them precious.

Incidentally, most of us are more or less familiar with the Old Testament story in Genesis of Adam and Eve and the serpent who tempts Eve. The snake has many mythological associations, though this is perhaps the most familiar.

The favoured habitat of the diamond python happens to be our region, the mid-north coast, as they love the warmth and humidity. They are in fact the most southerly pythons in the world, however, and used to be found quite frequently in parts of Victoria, especially East Gippsland. I say used to because the numbers in Victoria have declined to the point where they are classified there as vulnerable.

Frequent bushfires, including the wildfire of 2019–20 which devastated much of Mallacoota and Croajingalong National Park on the Victoria/NSW border, have obviously been a factor. Even here, in their preferred habitat, numbers are thought to be declining, which is likely why they sometimes interbreed with the hardier carpet python. This hybridisation may explain the variation in pattern markings on their skins. Of course, variations occur within any species, so interbreeding is not necessarily the reason. As always, any changes in natural habitat are inseparable from species changes – something to be explored later.

Diamond pythons may look dangerous, yet they are generally quite harmless to humans, only biting (and then not with serious consequences) if threatened or cornered. As we found with our two-day guest, they behave as if humans don't exist. A small baby left alone in a bassinet or Moses basket may be a different thing – but what mother would leave a newborn alone outdoors, anyway!

Diamond pythons are considered the most placid of all Australian snakes. Their preferred diet consists of possums, flying foxes (where available, such as in Bellingen, where there is a fox camp), birds of various sizes and rodents. Cats and small dogs are also acceptable, however, so letting them free range around a densely vegetated garden will likely put them at risk. The diamond python young, who are surprisingly small at birth, exist almost entirely on skinks and other small lizards, with larger prey being introduced into their diet as they grow.

Looking at the size of a diamond python's head, it seems surprising they can devour large prey like possums and small dogs. But they not only have teeth (a whole hundred and fifty of them, backwards-pointing) with which to seize their prey, they also have a lower mandible with the capacity to temporarily dislocate, expanding to accommodate a giant mouthful, then contracting, repetitively. Their prey will then be gradually suffocated when the snake coils around it and squeezes it to death. This is the diamond python's sole means of killing.

The process of digestion is often very slow – sometimes even a couple of weeks. Because digestion is such a slow process, the prey can actually decay before being digested, which can occasionally result in the

A diamond python suffocating its prey (sadly, a king parrot), showing the expanding jaw starting to absorb it, head first.

snake itself being poisoned by its own prey. Our courtyard visitor stayed as long as it did because it was still in the process of digesting its large meal, so disinclined to move about.

Diamond pythons are muscular and usually slow-moving anyway, except when seizing prey. They generally move during the day, perhaps as little as a hundred metres between prey targets. They don't hunt in the prowling sense, though; they capture their prey by ambush, lying perfectly still, sometimes for several weeks, till a suitable target comes within range. Then they move with sudden rapidity. Because they do most of their ambushing at night, they have heat-receptors which help them spot a prey target in the dark.

They are sometimes sighted close to homes in our subtropical part of the world, even in roof cavities, probably because of the likelihood of vermin there. A friend of mine and her family living in a rammed-earth home just out of town noticed an awful smell which worsened by the day. Then they noticed dark drops of a foul-smelling liquid seeping from the ceiling onto their kitchen bench. Eventually, they discovered the problem: a diamond python had died in their roof-cavity. By this time, they were on the point of evacuating to escape the vile stench. A phone call solved the problem, but even with all the windows open, the smell still took days to dissipate. Such events are fortunately rare.

Snakes are classified as middle-order predators and, like every other living creature, play a vital role in maintaining eco-balance. The diamond python's diet can help keep other predators in check just as they, too, can be predated upon by raptors and even kookaburras. Obviously a mature diamond python would be beyond the capacity of such predators; it's their young that often fall victim to the these predators – another reason why nature endows the female with such large clutches.

The reason people occasionally spot them close to their home is that vermin also tend to hang around humans for the food potential we unintentionally offer them – almost certainly the reason for our visitor. The fact that we have spent almost three years here evidently vermin-free may well be, in part, thanks to a resident diamond python or two.

An adult diamond python coiled on open ground, so naturally camouflaged that it's hardly surprising people rarely see them in their gardens.

They are secretive creatures, and their camouflage markings make them cryptic, so although they may be inhabiting your garden, they are rarely seen. This also makes it hard for scientists to monitor their numbers and behaviour; hence the use of telemetric radio tracking devices attached to those they find, to provide information about their habits, behaviour and diet. Estimating their numbers is more difficult.

Diamond pythons are oviparous: that is, they lay eggs, which the female coils around in deep leaf litter to keep them warm until they hatch in six to eight weeks, occasionally 'shivering' to distribute the heat more evenly. In clutching their eggs like this, diamond python females are more nurturing than most other reptiles, though they typically abandon their progeny once hatched.

The eggs are oval in shape, with a hard, leathery shell which allows gas and moisture exchange between the embryo and the outside world. Unlike many reptiles, and more akin to birds, the young have an egg-tooth at the end of their snouts with which to crack open their shell at birth. The female will be so vigilant that she will not eat during the whole gestation period. Females only reproduce about every third year, so it makes biological sense that they lay between nine and fifty-four eggs each time. The survival rate of the young is also undermined by predators such as red foxes and cats, as well as native predators, because they are only forty to fifty centimetres in length when hatched.

Mating takes place in early spring. The female will lay a scent trail to lure male suitors and typically, a group of males will hang around one female for up to eight weeks touting for supremacy. Since she may mate with several suitors, the progeny will likely have mixed parentage – fortunately free of the moral and legal issues this would pose in a human situation. Her eggs will be laid in early summer, hatching normally occurs some time during autumn. Adult diamond pythons grow to between two and three metres and it is believed they can live to a hundred years, though the average is closer to twenty years.

Like every creature in the natural world, any major change to their

A diamond python in the process of suffocating a hapless pet rabbit.
The snake's head is lining up for the jaws to expand and begin to crush it.
It will probably take days to digest this large meal,
but may not eat again for weeks.

normal habitat will have detrimental effects on them. The focus in this chapter is on our region, the mid-north coast of NSW, but a report released by the National Conservancy Council on 28 June 2019 helps highlight the scale of change happening to natural wildlife habitat by forest logging alone. Tree-clearing in our state has tripled during the last five years, accelerated by the state government's relaxing of land-clearing laws in November 2017. Under this ill-advised dispensation, loggers and farmers now have legal approval to clear extensive additional bushland. Obviously, this threatens the lives of vast numbers of creatures. Clearing is a major cause of disturbed habitat, but by no means the only threat the diamond pythons and other fellow creatures have to contend with.

Diamond pythons prefer a well-vegetated environment, especially in rainforest such as ours, though they do live happily in woodlands and forests further in from the coast. As mentioned earlier, sightings in Victoria, which occur mainly in East Gippsland, are becoming rarer. They are not yet classified on the mid-north coast as endangered, but their numbers appear to be declining. Locals report fewer sightings.

Broadly speaking, forest-clearing poses the biggest threat. Not only does this destroy the natural habitat of diamond pythons, along with that of many other species; it also leads to rising temperatures, further compromising their survival. Add to this the devastation caused by bushfire and the effects of ill-timed back-burning in the name of fuel reduction, as well as more frequent roadkill as the growing human population creates more road traffic.

The first white settlers were fascinated by all the strange new creatures living here, but, not content just to draw and observe, thought nothing of killing them. We read of such practices with horror, yet need to know the illegal capture of snakes and other creatures by smugglers and pet market suppliers still goes on. There's big money in it, and the beautiful, benign diamond python is a particular target. As mentioned, being middle-order predators, diamond pythons do have natural predators such as large raptors, or birds like kookaburras in the case of their young, but the introduction of European species such as red foxes and cats has exacerbated the scale of predation of young diamond pythons, thereby upsetting the delicate ecological balance.

It isn't hard to see that all these threats are interconnected and almost entirely traceable to the impact of white occupation. The original human inhabitants worked within the natural order, based on survival, not greed. As writers like Bruce Pascoe (*Dark Emu*, especially) show, Indigenous peoples were far more sophisticated and skilled than it suited earlier settlers to acknowledge, and today, as we face imminent climate disaster globally, there is much we could learn from their deep knowledge of our natural environment.

This chapter is a plea – one of many, many now – that we learn about our disappearing fellow creatures, exercise wisdom in respecting their right to life and do all we can to save what's left of their homes before it is too late. The diamond python has a right to life equal to ours, and its likelihood of survival as a species is now more than ever in our hands. Not only is it a beautiful creature, but one of awe-inspiring antiquity. This was the diamond python's environment long before it was ours.

Sea Life in Strife

It was David Attenborough who first made me aware that our marine environment is every bit as important as our earthly one, comprising 70% of the planet's surface.

The extraordinarily rich marine flora biota is precious and fascinating in itself, but it also has an interconnected, symbiotic relationship to life on land. When we speak of climate change – as we must – we need to recognise that melting ice and rising temperatures affect the sea as well, and that there are many species at increasing risk of extinction under water that are quite as important as those on land.

It's not just that water covers a wider surface area of the planet than land; that surface needs to be multiplied by the depth of oceans and rivers. We've all heard and seen images of the stunning Great Barrier Reef, and possibly been lucky enough to visit there before the awful bleaching began. Not only has it been one of the great wonders of the world; it is a vital ecological environment. Beneath the waters of the world are vast, complex ecosystems which are exquisitely beautiful; they also have interconnections with land.

This chapter can't hope to do justice to the complexity of this underworld. My plan is to focus on a few species, both because they are fascinating and because they play pivotal roles in the marine ecology. The species included here also happen to be vulnerable, in need of our protection. Again, though the focus will be mainly on the mid-north coast of NSW, the trends are generally not confined to this region.

I'd like to start with sharks (*elasmobranchs*). I was amazed to discover that we have over three hundred shark species in Australia and that they actually have more in common with whales and dolphins (which are mammals) than they do with other fish.

For one thing, they have side and dorsal fins and a torpedo-like body, like dolphins; like whales, they are totally ocean-dwelling and have a single tail fin for propulsion. Sharks also differ distinctly from fish in that the latter have bone skeletons, whereas a shark's body is constructed of cartilage. Unlike fish, too, sharks have teeth of varying designs to suit their dietary needs. These teeth are frequently replaced throughout their lives. They are classified as cartilaginous fish, reflecting their unusual complexity as a genus. Globally, they currently represent 1% of the total fish population.

Sharks are ancient creatures. They have been in existence for at least four hundred and twenty million years, meaning that they pre-date dinosaurs, humans and even trees. They have survived four of the mass extinctions. Yet today – during the Anthropocene (or human) era – their numbers are clearly in decline, some critically, in ways and for reasons we will look at here. We can't allow this trend to continue. Not only do they play a vital role in the marine ecosystems such as coral reefs; their sheer antiquity is reason enough to fight for their survival.

Most of us are deeply afraid of sharks. My partner has admitted to shark-nightmares, and he wouldn't be alone. Yet the reality isn't nearly as fearsome. In the Pacific Ocean along the mid-north coast, we have only three species of shark known to prey on humans: the great white shark, the bull shark and the tiger shark, and even among these species, attacks are extremely rare and often human-provoked. We are not their diet of choice!

You may have heard of the Australian scuba-diver Valerie Taylor, whose skills also include writing, painting, documentary-making and marine conservation work. The now-eighty-five-year-old was inter-

Grey nurse shark.

Tiger shark.

viewed in January 2000 in connection with a new documentary about her life. She spoke passionately about the alarming drop in shark numbers, including the great white and tiger species, respectively now 92% and 74% gone from Australian waters. No doubt finning (to be mentioned later), large-scale fishing and increasing water temperatures are major causes.

She argues we have an exaggerated fear of sharks, which feel with their teeth and would most likely simply back away if you remained perfectly still. And most of them are harmless, anyway. I'm inclined to maintain a healthy respect all the same.

But it does seem we are overly fearful of these magnificent creatures. The odds of being killed by a shark in Australian waters have been estimated at one in eight million. Most sharks won't attack humans unless threatened: like us, they are hard-wired to the fight or flight response. We need to move beyond this phobia to confront the sad truth that our magnificent sharks are under threat worldwide as a result of human activity.

As our keystone marine species and apex ocean predators, sharks play a vital role in maintaining a healthy balance in our reef and underwater ecosystems. Most sharks feed on fish, though the larger species include marine mammals such as dolphins, seals, turtles and even seabirds in their diet. The bull shark will also happily include other, smaller sharks. Surprisingly, the largest shark, the whale shark, prefers to live on plankton – no doubt in large quantities!

Sharks are mostly quite long-living, but are slow to mature. Many of them are also low in fertility, having few offspring and breeding irregularly. This alone puts them at risk of extinction over time. They can be either oviparous (egg-laying) or viviparous (live-bearing). On the mid-north coast we have both. This, combined with all the human-caused damage, makes it vital that we do all we can now to conserve our shark species. As our apex marine predators, it is their feeding needs which maintain the balance of all marine life below them in biodiversity terms. They keep the seabed clean by consuming weak and sick creatures; they do the same for our precious coral reefs. A drop in their numbers therefore is shown to have a serious impact on the whole marine ecosystem.

Here's an example (it happens to be from studies in Hawaii, but is happening here too): loss in shark numbers has led to an oversupply of turtles, which have consequently been over-grazing the seagrass floor, thereby destroying their own habitat. This naturally sets up a chain impact on the whole marine life infrastructure.

There are approximately four hundred and forty shark species globally, three hundred of which are found in Australian waters, either year round or seasonally. Of these, seventy are variously classified as at risk of extinction on current trends. In the waters of the mid-north coast, as at 2000, the grey nurse shark (*Greharias Taurus*) and the speartooth (*Glyphis glyphis*) were already critically endangered; the Northern Rivers shark (*Glyphis garrick*) was considered endangered and in the vulnerable category were great white sharks (*Carcharodon leucas*), the whale sharks (*Rhincodon typhis*) and dwarf sawfish sharks (*Dindagubba*).

These are figures from twenty years ago: the situation is far worse now. We need to face the fact that this rapid downward trend is directly related to human behaviour, in ways we will look at shortly. Fortunately, there are international agreements in place to liaise with Australia and other affected countries. For instance, Australia has been a signatory to the Conservation of Migratory Species of Wild Animals since 2011, and was the third country to join.

The fate of great whites (the world's largest flesh-eating sharks) is particularly concerning not only because of its important role in keeping the reefs clear of decay and debris, but also because their breeding habits are not conducive to numbers survival even without further threats. The fact that they are low in fecundity, slow to mature and only breed about every sixteen years, and a female producing an average of only ten progeny at a time, their sharp decline in numbers is now especially critical.

Little is known about the breeding behaviour of sharks in general, though a nursery of some great whites was found fairly recently at Port Stephens, at the southern end of the mid-north coast. They are quite nomadic, having no fixed address, in our region following the food chain extensively along the eastern coastline between Wilson's Promontory, Victoria, and the central Queensland coast.

Great white shark.

Tagging and tracking are not new among marine biologists; what is quite new is genetic testing. Using this, CSIRO experts have been able to estimate that we now have only about seven hundred and fifty adults along this whole coastline. An interesting fact about the great white is that it has only monochromatic vision because it normally lives at a depth of about one kilometre, and colour is filtered out in deep water. Another fascinating fact is that these sharks may help scientists find a cancer cure; their genes protect them from cancer and other diseases and also help them heal quickly.

Grey nurse sharks are facing a similar plight: slow-developers and breeders whose numbers are diminishing rapidly, they have been classified as critically endangered since 1994. Beautiful creatures, they pose no threat to humans and are equally important in maintaining a healthy balance in the marine ecosystem. And so the story goes. All the sharks found in the waters of eastern Australia are increasingly under threat of extinction sooner rather than later.

So why is this? There are several main reasons, all of them directly or indirectly related to human behaviour. Some of them apply to marine life broadly; others relate more specifically to sharks. Finning is one of the latter. If you haven't heard of it, expect to be horrified!

This barbaric practice involves catching live sharks, cutting off their fins (mainly for the Asian food markets, which regard fins as a delicacy) and dropping them back into the water, where they are left to die in agony at the bottom of the ocean. It is supposedly banned, but still happens in Australia, particularly in the northern waters.

It is still permissible to use dredging or bottom-trawling practices on a quota basis where the purpose is for human food as well as fins. So think carefully before buying flake in a fish 'n' chip shop!

Overfishing is obviously a problem too, both commercially and recreationally. The practice of exporting live fish, especially reef-fishing, to Asian countries such as China is harmful to sharks and all the reef dwelling subspecies existing with them symbiotically. And by-catch (sharks and other fish species caught in nets incidentally when fishing for other species) is another problem. Like dredging or bottom-trawling, it is wasteful and damaging.

Less directly, but every bit as harmfully are the effects of increasing numbers of humans flocking to the coast either on holiday or permanently, giving rise to extensive coastal development and resulting in habitat degradation along the coast. Rising levels of atmospheric carbon dioxide have been occurring in the world's oceans since pre-industrial times, but are now causing serious ocean acidification.

Some marine creatures will probably adapt better than others – the details are not yet clear, but studies by experts in 2009 suggest troubling changes are occurring in phytoplankton and zooplankton, which is a huge concern for the health of the ocean. Now that most marine life is under threat, exploitative human behaviour is in drastic need of change. Fortunately, organisations are working to achieve this: Marine Conservation Australia is a stand-out example, but there are many. Look them up, if you'd like to become involved.

Let's look now at oysters. Like you, no doubt, my first thought was of the Sydney rock oysters I remember eating years ago. Before I started researching them, that is. But I was amazed to learn just how important a role the oyster has played in maintaining the health of our marine ecology. Marine biologists have become super-aware of what their seriously threatened status means to the whole marine environment and are taking major steps to reinstate some of the lost shellfish reefs.

Important work is being done by Nature Conservancy Australia, in consultation with Indigenous Australians (some of whom still retain much of the earlier knowledge), to replace some of the reefs exploited by the actions of earlier settlers whose practices are now being curtailed and steps taken to rectify the damage – which we will come to shortly. An article by James Bradley (*The Monthly*, February 2021) provides the most condensed up-to-date coverage of the plight and importance of oysters in Australia.

But first, why are they so important? One of their roles is water purification. A single oyster can filter up to a hundred litres of seawater a

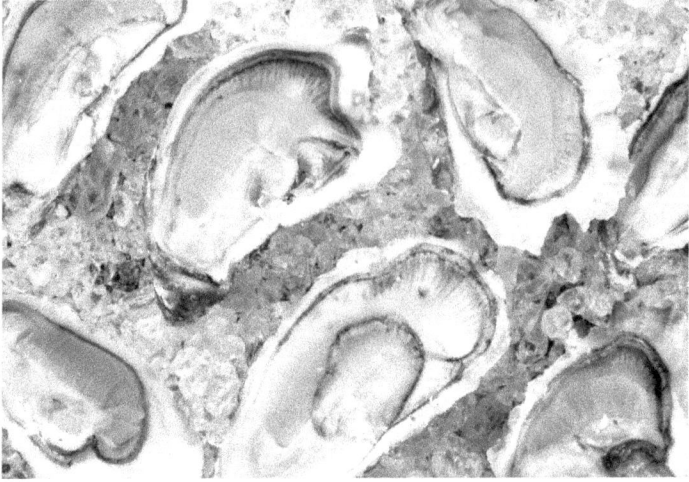

Opened Sydney rock oysters.

day. The organic matter they filter out (sediment and phytoplankton mainly) is consumed, causing pseudofaeces to sink to the seabed to feed crabs, shrimps and invertebrates. They in turn nourish the higher-order fish species. So oysters are the very foundation of this chain.

This process also effectively cleanses the water, allows sunlight through to improve the health of marine life and plants such as seagrass. A reef comprises countless individual oysters, whose shells pile upwards along the coastline. In the same article, Bradley cites an example in Port Phillip Bay: one hectare of oyster reef can filter 2.7 billion litres of seawater per annum, generating three hundred and seventy-five kilograms of fish. Don't underestimate the humble oyster!

Oyster reefs are formed a bit like coral ones. The world-famous Great Barrier Reef which stretches along the north coast of Queensland is obviously outside the range for our purposes, but makes a fascinating, if rather depressing study you might like to read about elsewhere. The Sydney rock oyster (Saccostrea glomerata), for example, creates a reef by piling cumulatively into a thick, vertical wall along the coastline. Another species, not found on the mid-north coast, but further south, is the flat oyster (Ostrea angasi), which forms its thick reefs from the sea floor. The nooks and crannies created by all oyster reefs support

Rock oyster farm.

abundant invertebrate-life: a single square metre of reef can support up to sixteen thousand such lives.

From a white settler perspective, oyster farming is one of the oldest aquaculture industries in NSW, dating from about 1880. But oysters have formed part of a healthy Indigenous diet for thousands of years, on a scale that didn't destroy the reef formations. They also made full use of their catch: the meat would be eaten and some of the shells then used to create fish hooks or cutting tools. If this interests you, I highly recommend a book, *Dark Emu*, by Bruce Pascoe (historian and part-Indigenous writer) – a real eye-opener about the richness of lifestyle of First Peoples in Australia.

Returning to Victoria from SA along a fairly treeless stretch of coastal country once, my partner and I stopped for a coffee break and, stretching our legs before continuing, we walked beside what turned out to be Aboriginal middens – remains of oyster shells from long ago. I felt in awe of that connection across time which one senses at such moments.

The favoured oysters to eat are the famous Sydney rock variety, found only on the east coast of Australia, and especially along the mid-north coast. Since the 1970s, overfishing for them and water contamination resulting from coastal development have together caused a marked decline in Sydney rock oyster numbers. Yet today the commercial Sydney rock oyster business is flourishing, thanks to man-made oyster hatcheries and farms.

On our coast, Sydney rock oysters comprise 67% of the total NSW aquaculture income, which in 2018–19 returned over $53 million. Much of this derives from export to China, Vietnam and the US. Most natural oyster reefs in Australia are gone (99%, actually) and the few remaining are found on our coastline.

This is tragic when you realise that oysters date back two hundred million years, and that one from that ancient time would look almost identical to those we know today – perhaps because they are so resilient. They evidently evolved from the first known molluscs, dating from the Cambrian period, about six hundred and twenty million years ago. They are an important but critically endangered ecosystem, the most threatened of all our marine environments.

Major restorative projects are under way. As mentioned, the Nature Conservancy NSW is constructing reefs to replace some of those now destroyed, especially in WA, SA, Victoria and Queensland. Wild oyster fishing is not new to Australia; it was thriving on a huge scale back in the 1850s. For example, ten tonnes of oysters a week were dredged from the sea in Western Port, Victoria – a process which obviously damaged the reef structure. Nor has the practice stopped: here on the mid-north coast in 2017–18, the oyster business fetched more than $99 million.

This reef reconstruction process can never recover all that has been lost, but it seems to be well worth doing and effective in those areas where it has occurred. Not only is this work helping cleanse the water; it also helps prevent algal blooms which destroy other fish and strengthens coastlines against storm damage and rising sea levels.

All marine sea life, both flora and fauna, is in decline now. I was surprised to learn that until recently, water creature studies focused only on freshwater species; a study dated 1994 was the first to include saltwater species (three sharks) – the remaining seventy included in the study were all freshwater species. Another study, concluded in 2002,

Short-snouted seahorse.

addressed the saltwater situation and discovered that thirty or so sharks and rays were already in need of conservation.

Today we know that even those extraordinary handfish (*Brachionichthydae*) – the seahorse, pipe-horse, pipe-fish and sea-dragon – are under threat. Of course: as in our forests and other land habitats, all marine life is interconnected and interdependent.

The scope of this book means we need to be selective about which species to focus on. But whales and dolphins (cetaceans) in the mid-north coast waters deserve to be included, I think, not only because most of us find them fascinating and endearing, but even more, for the significant roles these species play in the marine environment.

Extraordinary leafy seahorse.

Amazingly, whales help provide the oxygen we humans breathe, sustain fish stocks and help combat climate change – simply because they provide nutrients to phytoplankton via their vast quantities of excrement which float on the top of the ocean. Phytoplankton are unable to access the ocean floor, though other sea creatures feed happily on any dead whales which sink to the seabed. Globally, there has been a marked drop in whale numbers since large scale whaling began, which has resulted in a huge drop in carbon storage. On a more positive note, the numbers of some whale species, in particular humpbacks, have increased since the end of whaling.

Dolphins, and their cousins, the seals and dugongs, are really small-toothed whales (*Odontocetes*, meaning, in Greek, sea-toothed monsters). Like whales, they are mammals, not fish; hence their need to surface for air. They evolved originally from mammals which had legs underneath their bodies. Dolphins are known to be quite intelligent, sociable and cooperative, both with each other and also humans.

Walking on the beach some months ago, we saw a group of half a dozen dolphins playing happily in the surf, and when a single human surfer left his mate to join them, it was quite obvious they were includ-

Bottlenosed dolphin.

Humpback whale and calf.

ing him in the fun. Whales, too, are intelligent and companionable, but we don't normally have opportunities to witness it.

These mammal species also have a range of clicks, whistles, squeals and other sounds through which they clearly communicate with one another. Though they are long-living (dolphins, for example, live from twenty to eighty years, depending on their size), they are slow breeders, producing only one baby and then only every one to six years. So this makes declining numbers especially worrying.

Whales and dolphins migrate seasonally. On our mid-north coast, we see whales moving north to Queensland and the Coral Sea around April, and welcome them back between September and November. There's something reassuring about this predictable seasonal journey; it's like watching a ritual drama, suggesting that all is well in the natural world. But it *is* under threat now, as we know, and we need to cherish it and do what we each can to preserve such precious natural patterns and cycles.

Various government-funded bodies such as Marine Conservation Australia have marine biologists and other experts working on conserving our threatened marine ecosystems. A NSW Biosecurity Strategy to cover the period 2013–2021 created a biosecurity act demanding shared reporting, supported by a responsive and consistent legislative framework. Hopefully this is working, though I can find no follow-up publication.

A biodiversity conservation regulation issued in 2017 advises people not to go too close to whales, dolphins, seals and dugongs, as this threatens them. Experts also now tend to oppose the practice of keeping sea creatures like dolphins in purely commercially driven parks. Such venues are being curtailed worldwide: the only two major dolphin parks in existence now happen to be in Canada, and in Coffs Harbour, near us – the Dolphin Marine Conservation Park on Solitary Island.

The focus seems now to be more on responsible captive breeding for conservation purposes rather than public entertainment and curiosity. There are of course smaller conservation parks along the NSW coast and elsewhere, but the emphasis now is more protective than exploitative.

As far back as 2002, the Natural Heritage Division of Environment Australia sanctioned the NSW Conservation Overview and Action Plan for Australian Threatened and potentially Threatened Marine and Estuarine Fishes. This was the first such stocktake and its findings were alarming.

The use of large marine parks such as that in Canada and our own local one in Coffs Harbour are important for their captive breeding programmes: as with terrestrial creatures under serious threat, they aim to keep a species alive. Large sections of ocean habitat should be set aside where there is no human threat (something David Attenborough strongly recommends), but the question that hangs there for me still is: what about rising temperatures? Obviously, only drastic changes to the way we live can help save our marine and terrestrial flora and fauna.

To Bee or Not to Bee?

The bees build in the crevices
Of loosening masonry, and there
The mother birds bring grubs and flies.
My wall is loosening: honey-bees,
Come build in the empty house of the stare.

'The Stare's Nest by My Window',
from *Meditations in Time of Civil War* by W.B. Yeats

Yeats's *Meditations*, published in 1923, enacts his inner struggle to come to terms with his horror at the violence of war and his acknowledgement that, as a poet, his role is one of contemplation and reflection rather than military action. It's a fine and honest work, and one of my personal favourites.

The poet's persona is feeling vulnerable both personally and because of the wider state of war and unrest: the crevices in the loosening masonry are both literal and symbolic. The bees here can be clearly associated with peace, fecundity, cooperative behaviour, energy, even sweetness. The poem comprises only four short stanzas. Using the repeated plea to the honey bees to 'Come build in the empty house of the *stare*',* the poet, through the very creation of the poem, pits these positives against the brutalities of war. His use of the bee symbol is perfect – an image of nature at work positively and interactively, so the very opposite of exploitation and destruction.

These honey bees (*Apis melliflora*) have been around for a long time. Like the ant, the bee evolved from the wasp, though later than the ant. Wasps (*Arthropoda hymenoptera*) appear in fossil records dating from the

---

* On the west coast of Ireland, *stare* means starling.

European honey bee collecting nectar.

Jurassic period, and apparently began diversifying around the Cretaceous period: ants first (about a hundred and forty million years ago), then bees (sixty-five million years ago). It's interesting to note that wasps have been found to be the first invertebrates capable of a degree of logical thinking. The capacity to infer that if A is bigger than B and B is bigger than C, then A must therefore be bigger than C seems pretty sophisticated, yet these early wasps have been found capable of such thinking. And because bees evolved from wasps much later, they can be considered more evolved. That such tiny creatures can apparently think is humbling. I read somewhere in an article of studies that show that bees are capable of distinguishing between odd and even numbers. Extraordinary!

Most of us – myself definitely included – tend in our ignorance to underrate the importance of our insect creatures. We think of wasps as nasty, stinging creatures and bees as not only important for the honey they provide us with, but as also likely to sting. So many crude assumptions!

Wasps are both parasitic and predatory, but they are important pol-

This wasp, whose forebears trace back to the Jurassic era, show some like-ness to the European bee, which is a descendant. Not all bees show such an obvious resemblance to their forebears.

linators, crucial to preserving certain plants from extinction. As for bees, they're really far more important to our environment as pollinators than they are as producers of the honey which humans extract for commercial purposes. Honey bees are what most of us first think of when we think bees, but in fact they are not indigenous to Australia. They only reached our shores from Europe in 1822, though their numbers and distribution have increased dramatically here since then.

Other introduced species are the bumble bee (*Apis bombini*), which arrived in Tasmania in 1992 but has spread rapidly since, and the Asian honey bee (*Apis cerina*), first detected in Cairns in 2007 and, by 2011, declared ineradicable, in both cases because of their hardy versatility.

In Europe and the US, the honey industry is now seriously threatened because of climate change, disease (in particular, the varroa mite, which has killed off many honey-beehives overseas) and colony collapse disorder, which has been on the rise since 2006, affecting increasing numbers. A somewhat similar situation has already affected New Zealand with the arrival of the varroa mite so Australian commercial apiarists are on the alert. In this chapter, though, it's not the well-known feral honey bees that concern us most. It's our own native bees.

As with honey bees, native bees are pollinators, meaning they exist in a symbiotic relationship with flowering plants. Anything affecting the food source of living creatures will inevitably impact them. Less obviously, perhaps, the reverse is true: if there are fewer pollinators, then fewer plants will be propagated. The impact of climate change here is pivotal. Hotter seasons and lower rainfall make living conditions for all living creatures increasingly difficult, and insects are no exception. As always, the numbers of indigenous flora and fauna species is already in sharp decline.

Launching into my research for this chapter, I soon discovered how complex a topic native bees is in Australia. As with other vulnerable species chapters in this book, the emphasis will tend to be on our own location, classified as subtropical rainforest.

Thanks to climate change bringing lower rainfall, unseasonable weather conditions and the massive wildfires of 2019–20 which partly impacted our region on a scale which firefighters here say they haven't seen before, this description of their predicament might now be an understatement. Nonetheless, though species details and population numbers and distribution naturally vary across the country, the underlying issues and principles seem to apply broadly throughout the country.

The volume of research material available about Australian native bees is vast, though much of it is at a scientific level way beyond my grasp – so naturally beyond the scope of this chapter. The role of native bees is simple enough: to facilitate in the propagation and preservation of a healthy biodiversity. Understanding and tackling the challenges climate change and other human interventions have created, the threat to our delicately balanced ecological environment is more complex. But first, some interesting facts.

I was staggered to learn just how many varieties of native bees we have nationally: estimates vary between seventeen hundred and as many as five thousand, but the consensus seems to settle at around two to three thousand. There are also roughly three hundred and fifty thousand native flowering plants in Australia, and 90% of them depend specifically on bee pollination.

About 10% of our native bees (*Tetragonula hockingsi*) are classified

Native drone bees at work on their hive.

as social, which means they build hives and are structured around a queen bee, supported by infertile females as well as the male drones who fertilise the queen. Having hives also means that they produce honey, though in small quantities compared to the introduced European honey bee. The bees in the social category are stingless and generally prefer a warm climate, ideally with humidity – hence their prevalence in and around our northern coast region.

There are eleven species of stingless bee, all tiny and black, and no more than three to five millimetres long. Because they pose no threat to humans and because the honey they do produce is delicately flavoured, they are considered suitable for home bee-keeping in northern NSW and Queensland under tropical and subtropical conditions.

Not all researchers agree we should keep native bees for honey harvesting, and it seems to me best not to raid their scant honey supplies, as they need this nourishment themselves during the cooler months.

Stingless bees are vital in being the only effective pollinator of plants such as macadamias, mangoes, watermelon, strawberries, citrus and avocados: apparently for these plants it is only bees from the stingless group which have the specific vibration rate to induce them to release their pollen. I learned this from a BSc Honours thesis/research project carried out by Terence Parkes (2016). He points out that these precious stingless bees are now under threat from a microsporidian parasite (*Nosema ceranae*), contracted from feral European honey bees (via Asian honey bees) as a result of shared pollination supplies.

Honey bees are mostly non-selective in their pollinating habits, which makes this a difficult problem to control. The effect of this parasite on our stingless bees is to reduce the lifespan of afflicted bees.

Exciting new research is creating life-preserving strategies across a range of human practices. One is the invention of mechanical bee pollinators: a clever way to control the varroa and Tropilaelaps mite which has infested honey bees extensively in Asia and threatens their populations here. Whilst this seems encouraging, I find myself wondering what the biodiversity impact might be regarding the species for whom bees were food.

The remaining 90% of our native bees tend to be larger (the largest being the yellow, black and green carpenter bees, ranging from seventeen to twenty-four millimetres long). These bees retain the stinger inherited from their wasp forebears, though they are rarely aggressive, using their stinger mainly for defence. They are typically solitary, not hive building. Among the better known varieties are the blue-banded

Blue-banded native bee.

bee (*Apidi amegilla cinginata*) and the teddy-bear bee (*Apidi amgilla bombiformis)*, apart from the three main carpenter bee types, but there are endless variations within these categories.

It's worth pointing out that there is apparently only one known killer bee worldwide – an Africanised honey bee (*Apis mellifra scutellata*) – which has spread to parts of the US. It looks similar to the European bee cultivated in Australia, so we need to be vigilant.

Being solitary means that most native bees don't create colonies, preferring simply to make individual nests or burrows in the ground or in small tree hollows, which is done by the females. These solitary bees constitute the majority of our native bees, and are all larger than their social cousins. However, there is a small category of solitary bees (the *Stenotritidae* family) which are tinier than other solitary bees and are specific to Australia, therefore having a unique pollinating relationship with specific indigenous plant species.

Native bees generally have hairy bodies and their dense sets of hairs (*scopae*) enable them to carry pollen to their nests or colonies. The design principles in nature are endlessly ingenious.

All bees are proficient pollinators. As mentioned, some, like the European honey bee, are non-discriminatory in their dietary preferences; others are choosier. The situation is complex, as I hope to show without going into too much detail. I was surprised to discover that introduced honey bees collect 90% of available pollen in Australia, yet they only actually pollinate 5% of our plants. This clearly has negative implications for the symbiotic balance between the indigenous flora and fauna in Australia – the plant/pollinator interdependence. Not a healthy situation.

All the same, mass honey bee deaths are occurring across Europe and the US, especially from what is called colony collapse, believed now to be brought on by the varroa mite, which causes the worker bees to lose their powers of navigation, to lose home. Although it has caused the loss of many hives in Denmark, the UK and the US, this virus has not yet been found in Australia.

Here it is our native bees we need to be most concerned about.

Though the loss of honey bees could become a worrying problem commercially should the hive-killing varroa mite enter our shores, it is the threats to our own species that are the real environmental concern here.

Though native bees exist throughout Australia, they are now in decreasing numbers, especially in the interior of the country; their preferred habitat is subtropical or tropical, with access to reliable water sources. Not surprisingly, then, they congregate around the coast and hinterland from the mid-north coast of NSW right up into the Northern Territory.

Moving as we did to the mid-north coast, we were not even aware of them at first. There were so many new species to discover, and some are naturally more evident. But I read, and we since observed, that they are most active in rainy, humid or early-morning dew situations, and that they actually make an audible humming sound. These small creatures play a vital role in maintaining environmental health and viability, some in more specific ways than others.

Like honey bees, many native bee species also pollinate indiscriminately, while others are more choosy. The preference of stingless bees for certain of our cultivated tropical and subtropical food trees and plants has been noted. The blue-banded bee, for instance, is a great

Blue-banded native bee.

favourite. While it shows a preference for lavender and abelia and the pretty but invasive lantana, it is also drawn to tomato flowers – all non-indigenous, which is interesting. It's a great favourite with food growers because it buzz-pollinates tomatoes, blueberries, cranberries, eggplant and chillies, which feral bees avoid. It's thought to be drawn to blue flowers, though this obviously isn't the whole story, given this list of plants.

Teddy-bear bees prefer arid, claypan conditions, so are not found up here, and the leafcutters (*Apismegachile*), which favour the leaves of roses, buddleia and bauhinia, are found throughout Australia. The carpenter bee varieties clearly prefer more tropical environments, so are still strongly present on the mid-north coast. The green carpenter bee, also still thrives along coastal NSW and Queensland, though logging is reducing their numbers, because eucalypt flowers are their preferred diet. The yellow and black carpenter bees are still found in large numbers, though they are subject to a range of threats, as are all native bees.

A yellow and black carpenter bee: one of the larger native bees, yet it sits on a finger.

These carpenter bees, like the blue-banded variety, also have the necessary vibrator buzz to pollinate similar plants and trees to those favoured by introduced bees, thus being forced into competition with them.

All native bees play important pollination roles in our delicate ecosystem, and all are under threat from various causes wherever they occur in Australia. Obviously this applies more to the coastal regions of NSW and Queensland, since this is where their numbers and varieties are concentrated. The balance of pollinating bee to suitable plant is critical. Where we live, in native bee favoured Bellingen, all the detrimental factors seem to apply.

One of these relates to the presence of European and Asian honey bees. The most obvious effect of their introduction into Australia is their competition for available pollen sources. There is also some evidence to suggest they are displacing native bees in their search for tree hollows. The European bees, for instance, are known to visit over two hundred indigenous tree species, and the Asian bees have shown themselves to be extremely flexible in adapting to changing environmental conditions – something that is bound to be a growing problem with marked climate change happening.

As if it were not enough to invade the normal pollination supply which is designed to work in a natural supply-and-demand balance, the introduced bees are responsible for at least two other detrimental side-effects. The first results from the introduction of non-indigenous plants. Because the bees are non-selective in their pollinating, they effectively disseminate introduced plant species, which soon become weeds. Agapanthus and lantana are examples of this. The other undesirable side effect concerns disease – a more complex and arguably even more serious matter.

Introduced bees bring with them diseases not known to the indigenous species, which are therefore naturally susceptible. (As an aside, this also happened with First Peoples, who fell victim in large numbers to diseases brought here by the colonists.) Apart from the varroa mite, thought to have been passed from the Asian to the European honey bee overseas and now potentially a huge danger to our native species when it reaches our shores, is the threat from the microsporidian parasite *Nosema ceranae* (again, passed from the Asian to the European honey bee) which is possibly already posing a problem for the stingless bees, causing reduced lifespan and foraging effectiveness as a result of spores picked up in shared pollination.

In the early stages of commercial honey production with European bees, these bees took pollen from both native (especially eucalypt) and introduced plants on an opportunity basis. But two things have been learned since: firstly, not only that the introduced plants spread rapidly, but also these honey bees were drawn strongly to native plants because they are more pollen-rich than their accustomed European species. This was found to have put pressure on our indigenous bee species, as well as contributing to the spread of introduced diseases.

Other diseases have already arrived here and bee experts of both the commercial and environmental kind are researching ways to control this. Cross-breeding is being explored in the hope of creating increased vigour and disease-resistance and many crop growers (canola, lucerne and so on) are deliberately planting more indigenous plants around the perimeters of their crops. There's money in honey – recent annual returns are around $1.7 billion – but the role of our native bees in keeping our natural environment healthy is arguably of greater ongoing significance.

The sad truth is that the numbers of both introduced and native bee populations are falling. Recent figures for European bees in Australia are not available yet, but it is known that between 2003 and 2013 there was a massive disappearance of their worker bees caused by colony collapse disorder outside Australia which could at any time threaten the honey bees here.

As for our own native bees, their numbers are estimated to have fallen by 40–50% since 2006. This could become a huge concern for our biodiversity. There are other detrimental factors at work, too, of course: the use of pesticides by crop growers and domestic gardeners;

the loss of habitat from housing and commercial/industrial development; but above all, the effects of climate change.

The apocalyptic wildfires of 2019–20 raged over vast expanses of Australia, destroying millions of living creatures and with their homes. More frequent extreme weather events – fires, floods, droughts and hurricanes – combine to hasten the death of old-growth Gondwana forests, damaging their ability to regenerate into the future.

All this is a direct result of climate change. Almost one in three unique Australian mammals is now at risk of extinction as a result of all this; an even more alarming statistic (worldwide) is that there has been an 80% decline in insect biomass since 2013 – only a few years. We're sadly aware of it here: not just fewer bees, but fewer butterflies, wasps, cicadas, flies, ants, mosquitoes, even spiders and cockroaches, each of which has a unique role in our fragile ecosystem.

In essence, the situation regarding native bees in Australia is traceable to the same fundamental problem. Before European occupation of this country, there was clearly a harmonious balance between species, both flora and fauna. It is the introduction of foreign species that has upset the symbiotic balance.

It's tempting to include invading humans in the foreign category, because although Indigenous humans did make their mark on the Australian continent, they did so over a vastly different time span and without the exploitative impulse which drove the much later European settlers who brought in all the invasive species.

We can't reverse this, but scientists and growers are becoming much more aware and active in attempting to create a kind of equilibrium out of the complicated environmental situation we now find ourselves in. We can all play some part in this, wherever we live, and we can all start observing the extraordinary living creatures around us. And here's something virtually all of us can do: create a hive from an old log for the stingless native bees to come and settle in your garden. Or at least plant as many indigenous plants as you can, instead of the introduced ones, aiming for year-round flowering.

Avoid all pesticide use, of course. And sit out in the garden watching them doing their thing for the preservation of our threatened biodiversity. Feel part of this precious natural world.

My partner and I have recently moved to the nearby coast and this is one of our first garden projects. Look up 'encouraging native bees' on Google – there's everything you need to know there. And become a volunteer with one of our wonderful organisations devoted to the biodiversity cause, such as Australian Conservation Foundation and Bush Heritage nationally or any of the plentiful state and local organisations, where you'll meet some terrific people. Doing something positive beats creeping paralysis.

Example of a simple native home garden attractive to both humans and native bees.

The Platypus and the Echidna –
Our Ancient Monotremes

Everyone – probably worldwide – knows about Australia's unique but now seriously threatened koalas. But for some reason, the equally unique platypus and echidna haven't captured our species' popularity ratings to the same extent. Perhaps it's simply that koalas are perceived as cuddly creatures, almost like teddy bears. The same could hardly be said of the echidna and the platypus, our two fascinating monotremes.

Monotremes are an ancient mammal order, characterised by being egg-laying and endowed with a single orifice for digestive and urino-genital functions. The platypus and the echidna are the sole survivors of what was once a plentiful order, their descendants having evolved from one of the oldest mammal lineages on earth. They are found only in Australia and parts of New Guinea, and are among the world's most remarkable and intriguing animals, as we will see.

The earliest known ancestor of the platypus dates from the early Cretaceous period (sixty-five to a hundred and forty million years ago) during the latter part of long Mesozoic Era spanning the period two hundred and fifty to sixty-five million years ago, when dinosaurs were still plentiful. This earliest platypus was considerably larger than our platypus today, but recognisable as a forebear.

Until the Cretaceous period, Australia, Africa, Madagascar, Antarctica and South America were joined as a giant supercontinent known as Gondwana. The separation of this great landmass left our continent with many species of both marsupial and monotreme, but over time the marsupials adapted better to dramatic climate shifts than the once dominant monotremes. Thus, today we have only two: the platypus

Platypus diving.

and its offshoot cousin, the echidna. And compared to them, we humans are mere upstarts!

Our understanding of the connection between the platypus and the echidna is quite recent. Evolutionary biologist Matthew Phillips, at the ANU, has studied fossil records and gene research which he claims now date the emergence of the echidna to somewhere between nineteen and forty-eight million years ago. Still very ancient!

On the face of it, the platypus and echidna are radically different creatures. We'll go into this in more detail shortly, but one of the obvious differences – quite apart from their vastly different appearances – needs commenting on here: the fact that one is mostly a water dweller and other a land dweller. But it must be remembered that the echidna evolved from the platypus, so it is hardly surprising that it retains strong swimming skills.

There's a local example here from a few years ago which seems to prove the point: someone out walking along the Bellinger River saw what he thought was a drowning echidna, so he rescued it, only to see it waddle straight back to the river!

Together, these two are the only surviving monotremes in the world, as far as we know, so extremely precious for that reason alone. It's likely that they are the only monotreme survivors partly because they happen to have such low metabolic and energy needs, enabling them better to survive extreme climate changes. It's a fact that, since the presence of *Homo sapiens* in Australia, 30% of all mammals on our continent have become extinct. Now both the platypus and the echidna are diminishing in numbers, which is why bioscientists are conducting surveys, especially around waterways in NSW, to ascertain the reality of their status as a means of trying to rescue them. Volunteer citizens have been called on to assist in this because both creatures are elusive, so the more watchers, the better.

Another interesting case of echidna research, based in SA, is worth mentioning. Commenced in 2017 under the supervision of Professor Grutzner at the University of Adelaide, this Echidna Conservation Science initiative analysed echidna poo and have made a significant finding. As the work of Matthew Phillips had shown, the echidna was a kind of breakaway cousin of the platypus, land dwelling but perfectly capable of swimming. What Grutzner and team discovered, through close study of genomic testing of poo samples across Australia, is that the X and Y chromosome structures of *sapiens* and echidna are quite different. In effect, this tells us that our (*sapiens*) 1:1 chromosomal sequence came about much more recently than we had believed. Even more like recent upstarts! This prompts me to make two brief comments.

Firstly, largely because of human behaviour, the ancient platypus and echidna are showing signs of declining numbers yet (to quote Grutzner) 'we are the custodians of these fascinating mammals', and research is helping us to play this vital conservation role better. Indigenous people had been doing this for many thousands of years, of course.

The other point worth drawing attention to is that, because echidna are extremely elusive creatures, researchers have had to rely heavily on volunteers Australia-wide to send in photos and poo samples from any sightings. The Australian total now stands at an amazing twelve thousand, thanks to volunteers, who were awarded the Australian Museum Eureka Prize for citizen science. Opportunities like this are available for any of us to contribute to such vital projects.

Our surviving monotremes are strange creatures, each embodying the features of more than one species type. And different as they look from one another, they do share some important features in common. Both, for instance, have squat reptilian legs, set squarely at the sides of their bodies, and broad reptilian shoulders, no good for fast running, but great for rapid digging or swimming.In the case of the platypus, the hind legs are rearward-jutting, making them useful as rudders in the water.

Both platypus and echidna have hair (hidden by spines in the case of the echidna), sweat glands, three middle ear bones and a brain area called the neocortex. Both also produce milk to suckle their young. Yet, like birds, they lay eggs, making them oviparous, though they suckle their young, once hatched, as mammals do. Being fur-covered and warm-blooded aligns them with mammals, but their reptile- and bird-like attributes make them too primitive for such a classification.

The fact that one is mainly aquatic and the other mainly terrestrial, but capable of swimming, means that they also bear some resemblance to amphibians. Mysterious creatures indeed! To cap it off, the platypus also has a bill and webbed feet like a duck, and the echidna, a beak-like pointy snout. And yet, for all their differences, it could be argued that these monotremes are classified as eccentric, distant cousins of the mammal family.

Let's look more closely at these two individually. First, the platypus (*Ornithorhychus anatinus*). The species has been considered endemic is not currently listed as being officially threatened under any national environmental law. However, as environmental scientists are now aware, this is far from true. And I'd believe the hands-on scientists over an of-

Underside of swimming platypus.

fice-based politician any day. Unlike most politicians, they are usually free of agenda. But more on that later.

Platypus are carnivorous, feeding on the plentiful supplies of invertebrates and aquatic insects found in rivers and freshwater streams. They make burrows along the littoral banks, which become their breeding habitats. I recall being mesmerised as a child watching the platypus at Healesville Sanctuary as they swam with such speed and balletic grace in their captive environment. They are long-livers. The platypus lifespan can reach seventeen years in captivity, though, like many creatures in the wild, the challenges nature presents usually mean a shorter life than in a monitored environment. Interestingly, they are evidently quite intelligent: for instance, if you hold one, it will run its bill around your hands to try and make sense of you. I remember learning this at Healesville Sanctuary.

The platypus is not a large creature: the adult male can typically reach one to 2.4 kilograms in weight and measure fifty centimetres in length; the female, 0.7-1.6 kilograms and forty-three centimetres. Interestingly, their forebears, whom they still resemble, were about a metre long. Platypus are mostly nocturnal creatures, sleeping a good part of the day in the chambers of their burrows. This is one of the reasons experts struggle to learn much about them, which has implications we'll return to later. The other is their shyness, which makes them elusive.

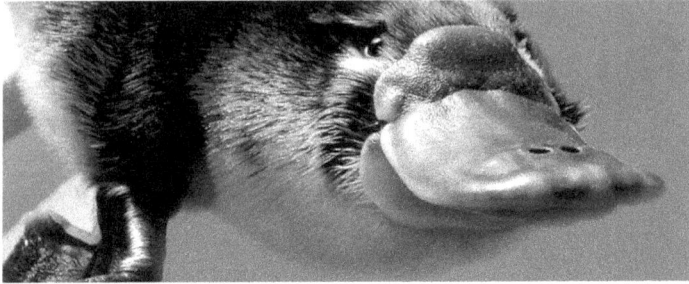

Close-up of face and bill.

Where we lived in Central Victoria before moving up here, we were sometimes lucky enough to sight one on our morning walks, swimming in and out of a burrow beside the creek – likely a female with young still in the burrow. Platypus are actually blind when under water; they detect their prey using electro-receptors located in their bills. Extraordinary!

Like their younger cousin, the echidna, they have no teeth, instead using grinding plates to eat. They must be pretty efficient plates considering their largely macro-invertebrate diet. As for their own predators, the young are subject to attack from large raptors and feral animals, but the most serious threat they face comes from our species, which we will elaborate on shortly, and which is obviously the reason their numbers are in decline. By way of defence, the male platypus does have venom, located in a spur on one of their hind feet, but this is used mainly as a weapon against male rivals during mating season. All the same, should a human be stung, the pain it causes can linger for weeks.

Mating season occurs between June and October, and at the earlier end of the season up here where the climate is warmer. Both males and females reach breeding age at around two years. Like their design features, their breeding habits are also a unique mix. A female platypus will lay between one and three eggs in her burrow, which will hatch in ten to twelve days. The young have a quaint collective name, a puggle, and will be raised solely by the mother. She will suckle them for three to four months – not via teats, though, but by a seepage method. This is apparently a typical monotreme feature. After this stage, the mother will leave them alone in the burrow for gradually longer periods, until they are ready to emerge independently and are able to swim.

But our rare and precious platypus has not had an easy run since white settlement, and its fate today is increasingly concerning. The first serious threat they faced came from early European settlers, who began trapping them for their skins back in the late 1700s – a practice not outlawed till early in the twentieth century, and even then, not properly enforced. There's a shocking record of a single trader who trapped and sold the skins of twenty-nine thousand of these unique creatures.

There's a case involving my own family which chills my spine to think about, involving a felt-backed rug made of the skins of forty-nine platypus. Its provenance was as a payment-in-kind from a grateful patient to my grandfather, who was a medical practitioner then based in Tasmania. It passed to my father, who confessed that he and his father had always felt uncomfortable about it. When my father died, it went (I'm not sure why) to my brother, who sold it to the museum in Launceston. In one of my online research sources, I came upon a large photo of a curator at the museum holding the unmistakable rug, which she stated 'was donated by a member of the public'. No doubt it can now serve as a shocking reminder of some of the exploits of early settlers who typically regarded all the new and strange flora and fauna as theirs to plunder.

Since that time, a number of human activities have impacted on platypus numbers, many of them occurring without our awareness. Platypus were once plentiful along the east coast from south to north, and also in coastal parts of South Australia. Back in the 1980s, some scientists spoke up about a noticeable decline in numbers, but nothing was done.

In 2016, Tiana Preston, an environmental water resources planner with Melbourne Water, observed a marked decline when she began her platypus study: she estimated a drop in numbers of about 30% since white settlement. More recent studies by enviro-scientists at UNSW (2019) assert that the decline is now closer to 50%. How did it get to this?

Because these shy creatures spend most of the daytime hidden in their burrows and research at night is difficult, the actual status of the platypus has been found to have declined significantly. Scientists call it a shifting baseline, as the situation tends to alter without our awareness.

Politicians – usually with neither knowledge nor experience working in the natural world, let alone genuine care – can claim what they like when challenged by environmental experts. The sad reality is that studies such as that by Gilad Bino (UNSW) tell us that the platypus is under severe stress, with many of their habitats revealing near extinction.'There have been especially severe losses in South Australia, and the platypus appear to have disappeared from the whole Murray-Darling Basin, where there have been no sightings for ten years.

Other human caused threats to our platypus include drought, feral pests and the usual livestock damage to banks along freshwater rivers and streams. We saw this also in the case of the Bellingen snapping turtle, you may remember. Both creatures build their nests in rock shelves or in burrows along these waterways, which are obviously damaged by cattle tramping to the water to drink. One conservation group at UNSW studying the platypus along the mid-north coast claims that they have all but disappeared from here. So the situation now is desperate.

Major threats also come from land-clearing and urban development and, indirectly, logging near waterways. Bushfire events are obviously damaging. Fishing, too, accounts for many platypus deaths: a surprising number of these rare creatures become caught up in the nets and traps set by freshwater fishermen. This is not especially an issue in our part of the world, though it's evidently a problem occurring in most platypus habitats. For instance, a local fisherman found four dead, caught in an illegal yabby trap in Braidwood, NSW, beside the Shoalhaven River, on 2 August 2019. So much for trapping being banned! Officially banned in Victoria and illegal in NSW, these yabby traps are still on sale in fishing stores in NSW, as I've seen in a store near here.

But perhaps the greatest threat our platypus face relates to water quality, which is becoming increasingly polluted as a direct result of human behaviour such as farming which involves cattle grazing and chemical sprays, and the continued practice of clearing and logging.

The rainwater which washes its way into rivers and creeks is often seriously contaminated as a result of chemical and fertiliser use. There's a fungal disease which has spread now from the mainland into Tasmania, where it kills about 35% of the platypus who become infected. The only reason it doesn't have quite such a devastating effect on platypus here is that they appear to have developed some immunity to it. But the platypus along the mid-north coast are suffering other forms of bacterial contamination. A few who were rescued recently along our coast were found to be riddled with E-coli and other infections. Their bellies were empty and two of them died the very next day.

For all of these reasons, this unique animal – considered (along with the echidna) to be one of the world's most remarkable – is now threatened with possible extinction unless drastic, immediate and sufficient measures are taken to avert this trend.

Like all living creatures, platypus have a place in the ecological web and a role to play in maintaining its health. Because their diet largely consists of aquatic invertebrates and lower-order populations, they keep these numbers in balance. Declining platypus numbers have created a growing imbalance, which has a flow-on effect. Damage to any living thing, both flora and fauna, in our finely tuned ecological system affects us too, of course, since we are an integral, and dependent, part of the whole, and not the owners.

Scientists are also discovering ways in which platypus can directly benefit humans: the milk females produce to suckle their young contains life-saving antibiotic ingredients, for example, and the venom in the male's spur can be harvested to help cure human diabetes. But should we be doing this? It makes me feel pretty uncomfortable.

So what can be, and is being, done to ensure that our unique platypus has a future? The need for a more rigorous policing of the use of nets and traps in freshwater ways is obvious. Restoring riparian zones near waterways, and banning cattle-grazing and logging close to these breeding areas would make a significant difference, though there is likely to be strong opposition from many where incomes will be affected. Creative solutions are always possible, though, with collaboration. Laws are not set in concrete and with climate change impacting us all, we live in a very changed world which is challenging us to seriously question current laws and practices. Bushfire events are likely to be more frequent and severe, as we're all realising now. Contamination of rivers and creeks resulting from this is inevitable.

There are some wonderful organisations such as Marine Conservation Australia and Nature Conservancy Australia and there's even an organisation called National Platypus Conservancy, as well as many smaller ones – all doing terrific work and all have supporters whether on the ground or financially. But the biggest difficulty they face is that the platypus must have uncontaminated water to thrive. For this, all the other problems need to be tackled, but we simply must do this. According to Bino and his fellow researchers, without serious changes in water and land management practices now, the likelihood is that the already diminishing numbers of platypus along the waterways of the mid-north coast, could drop by as much as 50% more during the next fifty years, even rendering these extraordinary and ancient creatures extinct.

Earlier in this chapter, I mentioned a citizen scientist volunteer research project concerning echidna, run by the Australian Conservation Foundation in conjunction with the UNSW. Only recently, I received an email from them requesting volunteers for a similar project on behalf of the platypus. It simply asks us to do the same watch-and-record vigil regarding any platypus sightings. I signed up for it. It's not much to ask, and again, when species numbers are now so low, the more people collecting evidence, the better our chances of saving this precious species. As it happened, we didn't experience any definite sightings where we watched, but even negative results help ACF to target their efforts to save the surviving platypus and look at reasons why they are not found where they formerly existed. There's so much you can do, wherever you live.

They have lived comfortably along our east coast environments largely unchanged for thousands of years. Their species took roughly a hundred and twenty million years to evolve, yet in the short two hundred and fifty-odd years since Europeans arrived here, it is now seriously endangered, though the government has yet to acknowledge the fact.

The echidna (*Tachyglossus aculeatus*) is also an extraordinary creature, developing from its cousin, the platypus, as mentioned earlier, so not quite as ancient a species as the platypus, but still a survivor from a far distant past. Like the platypus, it is a warm-blooded creature, and totally unrelated to the European hedgehog.

The long-beaked echidna was much bigger than the short-nosed species, but is already extinct in Australia (not yet in New Guinea). The short-nosed version comes in four different forms, but with only slight variations according to its habitat. This short-nosed species is therefore the creature we will be talking about here. It can grow up to forty centimetres and weigh up to seven kilograms, though its average weight ranges between two and five kilograms. Together with the platypus, it is the only mammal in the world which lays eggs – the only survivors of the once-prolific monotremes.

Echidna showing feet, 'beak', spines and walking movement.

Like the bill of the platypus, the echidna's beak is a bird-like feature. The echidna uses this to probe into rotting logs in search of termites. Its long, sticky tongue is about seventeen centimetres long – perfect for slurping up ants and other ground-dwelling insects. Its keen sense of smell enables it to find both mates and food. Add to this four strong, short legs and shovel-like claws with which to dig its burrow in the ground, as well as crumbling rotting logs for termites, and we have a creature well-equipped to live comfortably in its natural environment.

Both the platypus and the echidna have mammalian-type fur coats, but in the case of the echidna this is almost hidden by the spines covering its short black-haired coat. The spines may look aggressive to us, but are there purely for its own protection against predators. They also serve to make it a widely adaptable species, capable of survival in habitats are widely diverse as desert and rainforest.

It seems to me – though I have read nothing to verify this – that the burrowing is something the echidna shares with its older cousin, the platypus. Male echidna also have a back-leg spur, but unlike the male platypus, theirs is not venomous. The fact that an echidna can swim with ease if necessary (a survival of its ancient kinship with the platypus) and can also burrow hastily underground in the event of a bushfire, for instance, lying low till the fire front passes and the earth cools, probably gives it a survival edge over the platypus, who simply depends on fresh, clean water. That being said, echidna are also slow-moving, which can place them at risk at times. We'll return to this soon.

An echidna normally lives about ten years in the wild, though far longer in captivity, where it is protected from the usual dangers all creatures normally face. The record age for an echidna living in captivity is forty-nine years! In the wild, the echidna is a wanderer, though its range is usually no more than a fifty-hectare radius. The exception is during breeding, when the female will stay put in the burrow for several months, until the puggle (Yes, that's what they're called. What a lovely name! Like an imaginary creature from a child's story, but this one is real!) is weaned and is covered in spines to protect it – usually at six months.

At mating time, a female will be followed by several hopeful males for surprisingly lengthy periods, and she will usually opt for the most persistent suitor. She will then lay a single, leathery, jelly-bean-sized egg and carry it in her pouch. Once it hatches into a puggle, she will suckle it for three months, still keeping it in her pouch, by which time it will have grown its protective spines. However, she will continue to suckle it till it is six months old, at which stage it is ready for independent living.

The echidna is a shy creature, like the platypus, so not often seen, but perhaps because of this the decline in numbers has apparently not been undetected until quite recently. Imagine our delight when, out on one of our littoral forest walks one morning some months ago, we came upon an echidna busily nosing into a rotting log on the path. Actually, we heard its scuffling noises even before seeing it. We froze and watched quietly, far enough away for it to be unaware of us, but I couldn't resist edging my way slowly closer.

I discovered that, provided I made my incremental moves while it was absorbed in catching termites in the decaying wood with its back to me, it was fine – up to a point. But a couple of times it caught me in the act, and instantly shrank into its spines. We think it was a young-ster, but there was nothing deficient about its survival instincts. At one

Close-up of echidna quills.

Echidna foraging for ants.

point, the echidna and I actually stared into each other's eyes, and I felt overcome with awe and an unmistakable sense of connection. I will cherish the memory.

My personal reading from the research I've done is that, in some ways, the platypus is more at risk of impending extinction than the echidna, because in the event of bushfire an echidna can hastily seek cover either in its own burrow or that of a rabbit or wombat, if need be, or even under rock ledges. The platypus seems more vulnerable because its main habitat, fresh water, becomes overheated and contaminated during bushfires, rendering it uninhabitable.

Even so, echidna numbers are in decline along the mid-north coast – which makes our fortuitous sighting even more special. It's vital that we do all we can to save them, both for their uniqueness and their appeal. I also want people after my time to have such precious opportunities to connect with our fellow creatures.

The threats to the echidna are similar to those affecting the platypus regarding habitat loss. For the echidna, it takes the form of diminishing fallen timber and understorey, thanks to bushfire and logging. The echidna also has to contend with attack by feral animals such as red foxes and cats, or by native predators such as dingoes and large goannas which are also becoming hungrier as their own habitat is impacted. But whereas the platypus must have clear, uncontaminated water, the echidna is at risk of roadkill because it is slow-moving – not designed to handle our fast-moving vehicles.

If you'd like to get involved in doing something to save these fascinating and unique creatures – keeping alive something of our own connectedness to some of our earliest forebears, there are many terrific organisations, as I mentioned earlier, both at state and national levels, as well as lots of local organisations unfunded by government, which are always in need of volunteers and donations.

To mention just a few: Australian Conservation Foundation; Bush Heritage; and there's even a dedicated group called the Australian Platypus Conservancy, located in Victoria, but available to support the platypus wherever they are located. There are many others, too, which you can easily find in a basic internet search.

To see either a platypus or an echidna close up is an unforgettable experience – something all children need to share. You are guaranteed to feel some kinship and to fall in love with these extraordinary creatures to whom we are, after all, distantly related. To know them is to love them, and to love them awakens in us the urge to help protect them.

Fragile Frogs

Frogs have been one of my favourite small creatures since early childhood. I have a vivid memory of being at a five-year-old friend's birthday party in a large park which had a creek running through a stand of acacias and eucalypts towards the back. While everyone was busy on the play equipment, I'd wandered off to the creek, where I found a tiny green frog on a rotten log. It was the purest emerald with a thin yellow line running along each side of its body, and the most delicate and exquisite long fingers and toes. Its feet, I saw, were partly webbed. I studied it, fascinated. My first instinct was – I admit – to catch it, but its little heart was beating so fast I was terrified of frightening it.

The future for these beautiful amphibians is now increasingly insecure, with herpetologists across the globe searching for explanations about the causes. One of the foremost herpetologists in our country is Dr Jodi Rowley, amphibian curator at the Australian Museum. Just recently I read a full-page article in *The Saturday Paper* (11–17 September 2021), reporting on the sudden appearance of dead and dying frogs (mostly, though not all, green tree frogs) especially around the Scott's Head area of the mid-north coast. The article quotes Rowley requesting locals to report any such findings to her to help them discover the cause or causes, as pandemic restrictions prevented her from carrying out normal fieldwork. She commented, sadly, on the significant reduction in frog noise across Australia over the past few years, but noted that the numerous recent deaths in our region is further cause for alarm.

Research has tended to focus on a condition known as chytrid fungus, supported by the fact that this disease thrives best at lower temperatures, and that warmer-climate species such as the green tree frog don't cope as well when we experience cooler seasons such as we have done for a couple of years now. The fact that post-mortems on dead frogs mostly reveal the presence of the chytrid fungus can't be assumed to therefore be the sole cause of death. Experts are now thinking there must be something else at work. The frog noise Rowley refers to is the male mating call, which is common to most frog species. Their recent silence therefore means one thing: no breeding!

Apart from being fascinating creatures, frogs play a specific role in our complex ecosystem. They feed on numerous invertebrates and insects such as mosquitoes and other disease vectors harmful to humans; they, in turn, are food for larger creatures. Snakes love them. So too do some birds and fish. I'll give you a first-hand example.

Last summer, we were given a large green tree frog discovered in a friend's vehicle as she was leaving. Without touching its delicate skin, we placed it in some thick greenery for camouflage. As we stepped back to watch it, a large kookaburra swooped from nowhere, and in one deft movement carried the hapless, squawking creature to its regular perch in the ironbark tree it had come from. We felt wretched, instinctively empathising with the defenceless victim, despite knowing full well that this is the way nature works. And the grim thought occurred to me that hunting and fishing as sport among our species are destructive practices our endangered wildlife can no longer afford. We need to reconnect with our fellow creatures in simply meeting our needs to help our planet recover the balance human behaviour has upset. If one species grows or shrinks disproportionately, then the whole fabric is distorted.

That species is us, as most of us now see clearly. What we need to face, if we are to preserve the delicate balance we depend on, is that we are not some superior beings with the right to use other livings beings and plants to satisfy our desires. We actually depend on them more than they depend on us. That point is worth repeating, because we are so hard-wired these days to the domination view.

Frogs are nocturnal creatures, which makes them elusive, so that declining numbers can be a hidden problem often till it has become quite grave – like the plight of the platypus. Finding sick and dead frogs

Giant barred frog.

during daylight hours around Scott's Head, NSW, was one of the signals alerting herpetologists recently to the fact that something was awry. Frogs tend to burrow into the mud and litter for cover during dry times – which, on the mid-north coast, is typically winter, when they are mostly silent. The loud noise of the males making their urgent mating calls starts up after the first good rains, marking the start of the breeding season. This behaviour is common to all breeds.

As I write this, we are having our first big rains for many weeks, and the frogs outside are proving the point. Let's hope it also means breeding! Fortunately, they can survive for fairly long periods in their burrowed, dormant state, but as our hot seasons become longer, dryer and more severe, the froggy breeding season is becoming shorter.

The number of frog-species alive today is staggering: globally, some four thousand have been identified (one report dated May 2021, claims the figure is more like five thousand), and of these, there are two hundred and fourteen species known in Australia. Sadly, though, there were actually many more: a 3.1% extinction rate was recorded during the 1970s and 80s globally, which equates to about two hundred extinctions. Yet there are species we have not yet identified and named that will likely be lost before we can!

It was a surprise to me to learn that frogs are actually one of the most endangered species on the planet. And it isn't only the prevalence of the chytrid fungus: in fact, this fungal disease is directly related to the contamination of our freshwater creeks and ponds, which in turn is certainly a significant by-product of human behaviour. Among the causes of water contamination and habitat damage are logging, building activities, the draining of wetlands to expand cattle-grazing enterprises, and also chemical spraying close to frog environments – there's plenty of that going on around here, as elsewhere.

Another problem for frogs resulting from human-caused climate change concerns their eggs. Frogs' eggs are usually laid in a frothy substance called spawn, in or near water and on the surface. Higher temperatures and harsher UV rays increasingly cause radiation damage to these shell-less eggs, which naturally impacts their breeding rates. Some herpetologists have noted a trend for increasing numbers of frogs spawning on land, presumably to protect the eggs from water-dwelling predators. But I wonder are they likely to be safe from land predators? Not an easy life for a frog!

The unwelcome incursion of the cane toad into NSW and even further south (Australia's only true toad. I wince at certain frog species being labelled with this ugly term!) is also having a detrimental effect on our precious native species by intruding on their habitats. Introduced into northern Queensland in 1935 to control the cane beetle that was damaging sugar cane crops, it not only failed in this purpose; it is disturbing the delicate biodiversity of our native frogs. Interstate invasion has proved hard to control, as the toads sneak in via timber loads, pot plants and even boxes of bananas heading south.

They have become a bit like the earlier introduction of feral animals and plants which have become rampant weeds threatening indigenous species. I was horrified to learn that, in spite of this, frog-harvesting is still occurring to supply the pet trade, despite the fact that they are supposedly protected by the 2016 Biodiversity Conservation Act. I'm not sure whether frogs are still on the menu in France. Let's hope not!

Water purity is vital for frogs. They have extremely delicate, porous skins which make their bodies susceptible to pathogens and chemicals. They not only have lungs, but their skins are also used for breathing and hydration in a life-dependent process called cutaneous gas exchange. This fact explains why many biologists and herpetologists consider water pollution – damaging this essential process – a likely explanation of extinctions which have already occurred.

This is no doubt the main reason why the croaking of frogs in an environment is an indicator that it's a healthy one and the thinning out of the welcome calls of hopeful males in breeding season is disheartening. The relationship between habitat and frogs is a reciprocal one of course: because the habitat is healthy, frogs live and breed there. Where

Australian stuttering great barred frog.

Our resident friend Groggy.

frogs happily dwell, you can be pretty sure this signifies a healthy environment.

We have evidence of this in our own lush native garden as I write. About ten days ago, we spotted a huge green tree frog on the bluestone pedestal of a sculpture in our front garden. He lay there seemingly comatose all day, then as the light faded, we heard his loud grunts as he travelled along the north-east side of the garden. He remained totally hidden under the dense ground cover and bushy native shrubs. In deep sleep. Next morning he was back on the stone slab. This pattern continued for several days, then he disappeared and no grunts. We assumed he'd become a large meal for a vigilant kookaburra. But no! This morning he was back on his resting slab, looking even more comatose (apart from the rapid breathing) and somewhat smaller. My partner solved the mystery. He remembered how in mating, frogs can stay locked in embrace for several days! No doubt the grunting will resume when he recovers!

Frogs are not just fascinating creatures; they are also surprisingly complex and play a vital role in the ecosystem as both food for higher-order creatures and consumers, for their part, on small invertebrates.

Their diet plays a crucial role in controlling such pests as snails, slugs and mosquitoes. Even at the tadpole stage, they contribute to the health of their habitat, with algae forming the basis of the tadpole diet of most species.

Field studies have shown that, despite the simple frog brain structure, they are actually quite intelligent in their capacity to process visual, aural and pain-related signals. As I mentioned earlier, it's usually the males who make the courtship calls we hear, which are surprisingly varied and in some cases quite song-like. They serve to alert females that they are available to mate, at the same time, defending their territory against potential male rivals.

Not only does each frog species have its own distinctive call; there are many dialect variations within this. A female frog will choose her mate by the sound of his call, demonstrating that she has the capacity to hear selectively and that she is discerning about her choice of mate. I find this amazing! We know that they are elusive and rarely seen, so it seems that hearing is their prime means of communication. Some frogs can jump twenty times their body length – the equivalent of one of our lot jumping thirty metres! It's interesting that in many cultures frog calls are traditionally regarded as good-luck signs because their mating calls always associated with rain and therefore fecundity.

Of the two hundred and forty-odd frog species identified in Australia, a surprising number still inhabit the mid-north coast of NSW: the bleating tree-frog and eastern dwarf tree-frog, Freycinet's frog, the colourful dainty tree-frog, the striped rocket frog, the whirring tree-frog, Verreaux's tree-frog, the tusked frog and the eastern banjo frog, to name just a few. These and others still have a likely future given no further damage to their specific habitats and hopefully some reversal in the water contamination caused by the clearing, development activity and chemical usage which has given rise to frog diseases like chytrid and other fungal diseases.

Apart from the virtual pandemic affecting mainly the green frog around the Scott's Head area, there is a growing number of frog species in our region which are currently classified as threatened or endangered. One is the green and golden bell frog (*Litoria aurea*), a cunning little fellow you would expect to be hardy, as it preys on other frogs which it lures by its calls. Unlike most frogs, which are largely nocturnal, this bell frog is active day and night, even basking in the sun!

The adults live close to the water in wet areas such as forest, swamp and soggy woodland, so their eggs and tadpoles are found in these watery places. The male makes its mating call while floating in open water: a long growl followed by several short grunts. We have occasionally heard this unmistakable call during mating season (typically between October and January) where we live, which is always heartening. The adults are quite attractive: bright emerald green to dull olive, with or without brown and gold blotches, about five to ten centimetres in length, with a smooth back marked by a dorso-lateral fold. Its habitat used to range along the east coast all the way from Victoria to Queensland, but its numbers are well down. It is now largely confined to the north coast of NSW.

The southern barred frog (*Mixophyes balbus*) is facing a similar fate. Once frequenting the length of the eastern coast of Australia, its habitat has now shrunk to the mid-north coast. It lays its eggs in shallow leaf litter or wet gravel, so longer winter dry times are obviously reducing its breeding season.

A similar situation is occurring with the delicate eastern dwarf tree frog. Once one of the most common species along the mid-north coast, it is now rarely seen or heard. Its welcome, sonorous and persistent mating calls after the heavy rains of the 2021 summer offered us some welcome compensation for the flooding of our burgeoning native garden.

The great barred frog (*Mixophyes fasciolatus*) is another frog normally thriving along the mid-north coast up as far as Queensland, but now seriously endangered. Quite a large fellow at up to ten centimetres, the dominant colouring is yellow-brown to copper-brown with fine black lines and a distinctive black triangle patch on the tip of its snout. Its fingers are unwebbed and its toes three-quarters webbed. It normally breeds between spring and autumn, kicking its eggs out of the water to attach to adjacent mud or rock faces. The tadpoles enter the water on hatching and live at the bottom till they reach 8.5 centimetres. From egg to adulthood takes about twelve months for a great barred frog.

Another whose future is now endangered on the mid-north coast is the emerald-spotted Peron's tree frog (*Litoria peronii*). Its call is said to sound like a crazy cackle but – perhaps not surprisingly – we have never heard it. Unlike the slow-maturing great barred species, these frogs reach maturity in 3-4 months, so presumably are shorter-lived. And there are so many others: the olongburra frog (*Litoria olongburensis*), the sphagnum, the Booroolong, the green-thighed, the stuttering and the Davies' tree frog, to name just a few.

All of these and many other precious species of frog are now struggling to survive in our environment. And why? It has to be stated that this crisis is one brought about by human activity. As I mentioned earlier, their incredibly fine, delicate, porous skins are part of their breath-

Freycinet's frog in Amplexus.

Davies tree frog.

ing apparatus, making highly susceptible to water contaminants. Any logging, clearing for building and development close to watery places impacts the health and safety of the frogs whose habitats we disturb.

The use of chemicals by farmers and even residents in their gardens for weed control is another problem – in this case, one we can control, so that the poisons do not enter the surrounding wet areas. Hotter summers also impact the survival rate of frogs, most of all because their spawn and eggs are becoming exposed to extreme heat, which can obviously destroy their viability. No eggs: no frogs!

We've already looked at some of the ways in which frogs are important to a healthy, balanced habitat. Not only are frogs food for larger creatures, but they have a vital role in maintaining the food chain. Even their tadpoles play a role by living on the unwanted algae in creeks and waterholes.

So what can we do to protect them? Even in an average suburban garden you can encourage frogs by planting natives (including lots of native grasses and ground covers), providing a water bowl or a pond if you can manage it.

If installing a tank is possible, this means you can keep the water up to your garden during dry times – the frogs will love you! If you happen to live in a totally man-made apartment block or townhouse, there are plenty of froggy groups you can join, probably not too far from where you live. It's a great way to meet interesting, passionate people!

If you have children or grandchildren, open their eyes to the beauty and mystery of frogs. You'll be doing both them and the frogs a favour, playing a vital role in nurturing our precious biodiversity and raising caring, responsible young people for a world that desperately needs them.

Cicadas: the World's Most Raucous Insects

I hadn't planned to write this chapter – I didn't want to overload you. But I read an article in *The Sydney Morning Herald* late last year that aroused my curiosity and have since done some follow-up research which I'm hoping might arouse yours too.

As a child, I was fascinated by cicadas anyway, and found them intriguing. They were such a presence in our suburban environments that they formed a familiar chorus in the background throughout the summer and early autumn. This won't be a lengthy chapter, but I simply couldn't resist sharing this. It happens to be high summer right now, and it's noticeable where we live that the familiar cicada drone which we expect to fill our summer days is quite sporadic and less persistent this season, so I wanted to find out why. But first, some fascinating background information.

Cicadas (*Hemiptera*) are a truly ancient species of insect: not (as mistakenly assumed by some) a member of the grasshopper and locust species, but rather a true bug, along with small bugs like mites, aphids and scale, despite the enormous size difference. There are over three thousand species of cicada worldwide. They occur wherever there is tree foliage habitat, whether temperate or tropical, though the more humid climates seem to be favoured. Australia is home to about seven hundred species – not all of which are even described yet, but numerically, we have the highest population of cicadas in the world.

Wherever you live, city, suburb or rural environment, you will certainly be familiar with that high-pitched, piercing drone that starts from nowhere and drones on seemingly forever, then abruptly stops – a chorus of thousands acting in unison.

Australian authority on cicadas Professor David Emery aptly describes them as 'the soundtrack of summer'. I'm reminded of Tolkien's elven chorus heard by Bilbo in the forest in *The Hobbit* (you very likely know it), which also started and stopped suddenly, its source remaining invisible like the cicadas. Perhaps Tolkien was inspired by cicadas he heard. If you've read *The Hobbit* or *Lord of the Rings*, you'll recall the chorus of invisible elven folk mysteriously stopping and starting in the treetops.

Maybe as a child you collected the fragile husks on tree trunks and on the ground under trees as I did, the shells the adult cicada crawled out of on reaching maturity? And the helpless horror when you witnessed a loudly protesting green creature (they were usually green) squawking in the beak of some predatory bird? This one is the green-grocer (*Cyclochilea australiasae*), the most common of Australia's species, the earliest known cicada. It's believed to be descended from the *Ci-*

Cicada emerging.

cadamorpha, fossils of which were found dating it back to the Upper Permian period about two hundred and fifty million years ago, when temperate and tropical climates began producing lush tree and forest-growth.

The life cycle of a cicada is extraordinary. The deafening noise we hear is produced entirely by the males of the species, turning on their most impressive vocal displays to attract a mate – in unison, I guess, because they are in competition with each other and have limited time to complete their life's purpose, but also perhaps, in the hope of frightening off their many predators on the safety in numbers principle.

Entomologists generally assume that the sound is produced by a timbal (or tymbal): a pair of ribbed membranes located at the base of the abdomen. Amazingly, every single male cicada has a unique voice (just as we humans have unique fingerprints, perhaps) and the females can distinguish between them.

Once mated, the female will lay eggs in the slits of tree bark. Once hatched, the nymphs, as they are called, will burrow into the ground, where they will slowly mature over a period of years – anywhere from one to nine years, depending on the species. They don't all emerge simultaneously, though every thirteen to seventeen years there tends to be a massive explosion of numbers creating an incredible din, capable even of damaging the human ear. At maturity, the nymph will dig its way out of the ground and climb a tree trunk, where it will metamorphose (crawl out of its chrysalis) and emerge as a stunningly beautiful adult cicada. Life above ground for the adult, though, is hopefully sweet, because it is certainly short. Its total purpose is to mate and reproduce, and to avoid predators long enough to do so.

Though there are distinct variations in colour, body patterns and size among the many varieties, all cicadas have some basic physiological features in common. Cicadas have two sets of wings: a shorter pair which fold neatly under the upper set, and an upper set varying in wingspan from 2.5 to fifteen centimetres. The wings are structurally held together by a pattern of veins, often quite beautifully coloured, like the

Recently emerged cicada.

insect itself – and seemingly colour coordinated. They have a pair of large, compound eyes set one on each side of the head, a well as three tiny eyes (*ocilli*) located on top of the head. Some, like the plainly named greengrocer, are simply beautiful. This creature has embossed designs on the head and upper body which look jewel-like against the vivid emerald green of its body.

Another attractive cicada is the double drummer. We have the body of one we found now sitting on a shelf in our living room devoted to

Greengrocer cicada, one of the commonest on the mid-north coast.

precious finds in nature, and even in death it retains something of its rich bronze and russet tones. The yellow Monday is another attractive one you may have seen. But there are too many to elaborate on here.

With a keen eye and much patience, you will eventually see a few, mostly dead ones not devoured by predators, but even live ones occasionally, though they are well camouflaged. As a child, I often saw them in summer, but I spent more time outdoors back then, and there were obviously more around than there seem to be today.

Cicadas have a simple diet: tree sap, from a variety of trees, depending on the surrounding habitat. On the other hand, they have all too many predators. They are food for most insectivorous creatures, including birds, flying foxes, reptiles, spiders (who poison them before sucking out the juices) and even wasps. There's a particular wasp in parts of Australia, the killer wasp (*Exeirias lateritius*), which cart them off to their burrows and store them on catacomb-like shelves as a larder from which to feed their developing grubs. So it is evident purely from a predatory perspective that cicadas are vulnerable creatures.

On top of this, their nymphs are exposed to risk from fungal diseases and even the effects of the magic mushroom psilocybin, a psychedelic drug used by humans. And in China, nymphs which make it up to ground level are prey for people who enjoy them deep-fried as a gourmet dish. The photo I saw of a cooked plate of these wonderful creatures didn't appeal on any level so I won't include it here!

One explanation of their emergence above ground as adults en masse is based on the safety in numbers theory. Some entomologists argue that this way, they can't be relied upon as a continuous food supply, merely a treat. The fact that cicadas are well camouflaged in sunlight – and most tend to be diurnal – makes them hard to see, and their sound, for all its loudness, can stop in a split second where danger is sensed, is also on their side.

Cicadas have an ancient history, like many of our vulnerable and threatened species. They appear in the music and folklore of several ancient cultures, ranging from Mexico to Japan. They are also mentioned in earlier literature such as Homer's *Iliad* and the writings of other Greek and Roman eras (Aristotle and Pliny, for example) and in the Shang Dynasty, China, between 1766 and 1122 BC. We newcomers surely have a role to play as their custodians.

They also play a vital role, like all living things, in preserving the essential biodiversity balance. Not only are they a food supply for many other species, but in living on sap, they effectively prune mature trees. The burrowing of their nymphs during their years underground helps aerate the soil, and their chrysalids and carcasses supply nitrogen to grass and trees, effectively increasing tree growth and seed production.

Obviously, climate change is impacting this already vulnerable species. Continued logging of forests, bushfires and flooding are becoming more frequent and severe, along with human over-development. It's even becoming apparent in built-up, urban environments, where nature-strips are giving way to inert concrete. The remaining soil is becoming compacted, so harder for nymphs to burrow.

Those wonderful big street trees I remember as a child seem to be disappearing in the interests of development. It makes me so sad to think that children growing up in the urban world, as most do, will miss out on the wonder of seeing and hearing these beautiful, fascinating creatures. Let's do all we each can, for both cicada and child.

A Way Forward

I debated putting a question mark after the title of this short conclusion but decided emphatically against it, because I am convinced that in a context as urgent as this – the future for living things on this planet – there is no room for a tentative approach. We are all fed up with promises, enquiries and political talk. I'm totally with Greta Thunberg on this. This kind of approach is doomed to failure when the task is as huge as the climate crisis we now face. The list of creatures facing threatened futures has grown alarmingly during the three years since I began this book, and especially in Australia. So, no, we don't need the question-mark!

The only way to achieve real change in the face of vested business, political and media interests whose aim is to divert our attention from this reality is to start the necessary action ourselves, as individuals and local communities. I include in this all those terrific organisations mentioned throughout this book as well as the numerous local groups wherever you live. It seems to me that if we want change *now*, that should be the starting point. The typical approach of bureaucracy it to respond to a serious challenge with a list of obstacles. Failure to act is therefore guaranteed! We need to start by committing to the change as a given, then think of the many ways in which we are all capable of helping it to happen – no matter how daunting the obstacles may seem!

A forthright editorial which appeared in *The Saturday Paper* (12–18 November 2022) strongly reinforces this. You may be aware of savage new laws recently passed in Tasmania (and the trend is spreading) making it a culpable offence to protest in public, however peacefully. This, in the name of 'democracy'. The editorial cites the example of a group of mainly young people resisting logging going on at Snow Hill in Tasmania – one of the few remaining habitats of the swift parrot as well as other threatened species. Bob Brown was there in support and, as police were arresting him, two swift parrots flew overhead – two of the barely three hundred left in the world. In his usual calm, clear way, he commented, 'There's a rising tide I haven't seen since the 1960s. Angst is turning into anger. The new environmental minister appears personally concerned, but the blunt reality is that as long as big money dictates everything, a single minister is powerless to stem the growing tide of climate disasters, which will relentlessly pile up as long as logging and mining continue.' By comparison, the 'positives' we hear about in the news are no more than Band-aid solutions. The truth is that those precious habitat trees currently being felled are the irreplaceable homes for seriously endangered species like the swift parrot. The future for the dead trees is as woodchips for China. Totally unjustified!

Not all of us can be environmental activists and may not even want to be. But all of us, as I hope you've gathered from *Let's Not Lose Them*, can play a role in helping to reduce our damaging impact on the natural world through modifying the way we recycle, adapting our lifestyle habits so that we consume less, wasting less and learning to be proud of being part of nature instead of plundering it as though we had a right. We are all capable of being better, and of being happier, more connected people as a result. Think of positive gain; not personal deprivation. Join local groups or bigger organisations and meet terrific new people; grow food and native plants as mini-habitats for our fellow creatures; involve your kids in the natural world so they can experience connection, not boredom.